the art of ballroom dance

793.3
F

dennis j. fallon
University of Missouri
St. Louis, Missouri

sue ann kuchenmeister
Winona State University
Winona, Minnesota

Burgess Publishing Company
Minneapolis, Minnesota

Consulting Editors to the Publisher:

Eloise M. Jaeger
    University of Minnesota
    Minneapolis, Minnesota
Robert D. Clayton
    Colorado State University
    Fort Collins, Colorado

Copyright © 1977 by Burgess Publishing Company
Printed in the United States of America
Library of Congress Catalog Card Number 77-70867
ISBN 0-8087-0632-2

0 9 8 7 6 5 4 3 2

TO OUR SWINGING STUDENTS

acknowledgments

The authors wish to express their gratitude to Mr. Paul Kuchenmeister for his excellent photography, to Debbie Fallon, Dave Strickfaden, Marta Royal, and Grayling Tobias for posing so beautifully for the photographs, to Mrs. Jo McDonald and Mrs. Jean Kustura for their typing and editing of the manuscript, and finally, to our students who inspired and encouraged our work.

contents

1

introduction

Judging from the increasing number of students requesting ballroom dance lessons, the growth of dance clubs, and the interest in higher levels of competence, the obvious realization is that ballroom dance is back. For those who recognize ballroom dance as an enjoyable recreational activity or a highly skilled art form, it endured the siege of fad dances of the past two decades. For those unaware of the enjoyments of ballroom dance, it succumbed to the free and uninhibited dances that were representative of our society's quest for freedom of expression. However, today's society beckons the return of the style, grace, and structure of ballroom dance.

What is most evident is the typically American demand for excellence. Students wish to become proficient dancers. An introductory level is satisfactory for a few students, but many desire a higher level of instruction. Hopefully, through good, sequential instruction, many students will retain the enthusiasm and skill to continue dancing recreationally, and some will pursue the challenge of amateur and professional competitive dancing that now enjoys international interest and recognition, largely through the leadership of England.

Numerous books have been written for beginning ballroom dancers. Typically, these books assist students in understanding and performing selected basic steps common to several ballroom dance forms. Unfortunately, at this level of learning, so little emphasis is placed on the technique and styling subtleties of each dance form that beginners never gain sufficient confidence, capability, or satisfaction to continue dancing on their own. This book focuses on a level of instruction that will provide students with confidence in styling techniques in several American and Latin American dance rhythms. In addition, this book should instill a desire in students to create a personal style and flair for ballroom dancing that may be enjoyed throughout life.

USE OF THE BOOK

This book has been written for the student and teacher. Possibly more than any other physical performance, ballroom dance entails the intermingling of the roles of student and teacher. The student constantly alternates in a role from student to teacher while engaging in the learning process. After receiving instructions from the teacher, the student enters a self-teaching stage, followed by a team-teaching period wherein the student and partner verbally and physically dance their way through each step. And surely the old adage, "a good teacher is a good student," is evident in ballroom dance instruction, since the teacher must attend constantly and patiently to the learning difficulties of the beginner and the desired individuality of the more advanced dancer.

FORMAT OF THE BOOK

The intent of this text is to progess students beyond the beginning level of ballroom dance, and therefore, it begins with detailed descriptions of the fundamentals of ballroom dance and systematically builds to attractive dance routines. In both novice and advanced classes, continuous, timely attention should be given to the basic fundamentals of ballroom dance. This is where the instructor of novice classes must begin; moreover, it is where the instructor of advanced classes must return.

The basic steps of each dance are presented initially in each chapter on selected American and Latin American dances. Following the basic steps are recommended step combinations for beginners. Each chapter then continues with advanced steps and concludes with suggested dance combinations for advanced dancers. For intricate dance steps that require additional clarification, sequential photographs are included to enable students to better comprehend them. This format allows the instructor to be flexible in regard to the learning rate of the class, and as a result, to constantly maintain a challenging and enjoyable level of instruction.

To further assist the instructor in teaching, each step is presented with three types of verbal cues. The *step cue* indicates direction of movement (Fwd-Sd-Cl); the *rhythmic cue* provides the tempo (q-q-S) for each step; the *foot cue* tells the dancers which foot to use (L-R-L). Certainly, efficient dance instruction rests on the instructor's ability to give precise cues to the class. So it behooves the instructor to know and use a variety of cues that will move the students individually and as a group.

Learning to ballroom dance begins with simply memorizing dance steps. Real enjoyment and satisfaction in ballroom dancing comes after considerable practice—when one begins to feel the mood of the music and to respond with aesthetically selected combinations of dance steps. Hopefully, this text will assist the students and teacher in reaching this goal.

fundamentals of ballroom dance

Because ballroom dancing requires a great deal of mental and physical awareness, the instructor should concentrate on fully developing the students' basic dance skills before progressing to advanced skills. Emphasis on style and constant reminders that a few steps danced well are better than several steps danced carelessly will lead to greater gratification for both student and instructor.

STYLING

Styling is the essence of dance! It is the characteristic expression given to dance through specific bodily carriage, clean definite footwork, body sway, balance, and the feeling and appearance of oneness. Through a relaxed, learning environment and precise demonstration techniques, the instructor must convey the importance of accepted style and the latitude for individual improvisation and interpretation in each ballroom dance form.

THE BASIC POSITION

The basic ballroom position varies with the form of dance. For example, the basic positions for the Swing, Tango, and Waltz differ considerably. The basic position for each dance is described at the beginning of the chapter on that dance. For the present, discussion of some points that characterize the basic position of the Waltz and Fox-Trot should illustrate our emphasis on proper styling.

In the basic position, each dancer's posture is erect with the hips forward, the feet close together, and the toes pointing straight ahead only inches from the partner. The man's left arm extends outward from a point between him and his partner. His left elbow is slightly lower than the shoulder, while the hand angles sharply upward from the elbow to a point level with his partner's chin. The palm of his left hand faces forward and holds the woman's right hand with her fingers placed between the thumb and index finger of his left hand.

The man's right arm slopes downward to the elbow which is raised to about the same height as the left elbow. The forearm angles downward below the woman's left shoulder blade with the fingers, grouped together, extending slightly downward to a point just beyond her spine. The man's head is upright and looking over the woman's right shoulder.

The woman stands directly in front of her partner, slightly favoring his right side so that she can look over his right shoulder. Her right elbow is lower than her shoulder and angles upward to her hand which rests comfortably in the man's left hand. Her right hand faces forward with her fingers placed between the man's thumb and index finger and her thumb gently folded over his thumb. Her left arm rests lightly on the man's raised right arm, while her fingers, grouped together, close over the point of her partner's shoulder.

In the basic position, the dancer's knees are relaxed but not flexed. The weight of the man is slightly forward over the balls of his feet with most of the weight taken on one foot. The weight of the woman is felt over her heels and is distributed primarily on the foot opposite the man (his right, her left).

It is essential to good style and poise that the dancers remain in contact with each other at the hips and lower trunk. Despite the students' initial reluctance to dance closely together, the instructor must constantly encourage beginners to maintain this contact.

THE WALK

Once the students are able to assume the basic position, commonly referred to as the Closed Position, they should learn to walk in this position. At first they will be stiff and uncomfortable, so the instructor must create a relaxed learning atmosphere while insisting on good posture during the walk.

As the dancers commence to walk, the man should establish a slight feeling of control over the woman by leading with his upper body. Their feet must move straight ahead and brush past each other on each step. Forward steps swing from the hips with the toe skimming the floor.

Backward steps also swing from the hips with the toe skimming the floor and the heel reaching backward to gain full leg extension on each step, thus creating a concave arc from the head down the back to the extended heel.

The woman's backward walk is basically the same in technique but much more difficult to execute. Because the backward walk is foreign to her, the man should always use his strong leading ability to help the woman maintain her poise and balance. When beginning to move backward, the woman's weight is shifted to the back of the heels before the leg moves from the hip. Here again the feeling should be that the body moves just before the feet. The left foot then reaches backward, transferring the weight to the ball of the foot, which permits the right toe to skim the floor as the left heel is lowered. The feet must always move straight backward without allowing the toes to point outward.

RISE AND FALL

Certainly one of the more pleasing visual aspects of good ballroom dance styling is the "rise and fall" of the dancers as they flow across the floor. This undulating motion is created by a slight stretching of the trunk of the body (rise), by a softening of the knee as it assumes the weight of the step (fall), and, for some steps, by rising on the toes. There are no sharp, distinct rising and falling movements, and the dancers should refrain from bending the knees to achieve this effect.

BODY SWAY

Another element of style is body sway which is used on turns, most noticeably Waltz turns. Although sways can be overdone, they are attractive and essential to good ballroom dancing. Body sway is accomplished by inclining to the right or left at about the center of a turn. Dancers will develop a feeling for the proper timing and amount of sway against the direction of movement, for it will add flow, balance and unison to their dance patterns.

As dancers delicately incorporate these elements into their technique, the gap between dancing and dancing with style soon diminishes.

BALLROOM DANCE POSITIONS

One of the distinguishing characteristics of an advanced ballroom dance couple is their smooth transition from one dance position to another. The changing of positions adds a new attractive dimension to ballroom dancing. Because this requires many hours of dancing together, the instructor should present these positions to students at an early stage in their instruction.

The basic ballroom dance positions are illustrated in the series of photographs that follow. In order to achieve a desired dancing style, some of the positions will vary slightly according to the dance form. These differences are described at the beginning of the chapter on each dance.

Full Open Position

Semi-Open Position

Open Position

Skater's Position

Arch Position

Wrap Position

Reverse Position

Closed Position

Sweetheart Position

Back-to-Back Position

Right Side Position

Left Side Position

One-Hand Position

Two-Hand Position

Free Position

LEADING AND FOLLOWING

In trying to determine why men have shied away from ballroom dance as an enjoyable recreational activity, one primary reason that might be considered is our society's misconception of dance as a "feminine" activity. However, there is another more obvious consideration: the responsibility of moving from one dance position to another, utilizing several dance steps in an attractive sequence, rests solely with the male partner. Combine these two factors in a tense environment where men struggle to save their masculinity, and the cause of men's apparent reluctance to dance may be discovered.

During the early lessons, the alert teacher focuses instruction on building the men's confidence. The teacher primarily does this by conveying to the women that they should be patient and understanding as their partners increasingly accept the responsibilities of leading. At no time should a woman anticipate the movement of her partner even though she may develop an awareness of his repertoire of probable movements.

Good leading requires firm control and proper position. Basically, the man leads with his body, moving his upper body before his feet. His right hand plays a significant role in leading the woman, while his left hand is used to guide and balance her. Essentially there are four leads: (1) the man's upper body leads the woman backward; (2) the palm of the man's right hand leads her forward; (3) the fingers of the man's right hand turn the woman to her left; and (4) the heel of the man's right hand turns the woman to her right.

Once the man knows the proper leads and gives them firmly, he must study each dance step so that his leads are timed to allow his partner to follow smoothly into the desired step. Typically, the lead is given just prior to the step. However, both dancers must be sure to conclude each step accurately before responding to the lead for the next step.

Although a man may begin to dance on either foot, each dance form in this text will be presented with the man starting on his left foot and the woman on her right foot. The length of the man's stride is regulated by the length of his partner's full stride.

BASIC BALLROOM DANCE STEPS

There are six basic ballroom dance steps that are used in most ballroom dances. Before introducing students to a specific dance rhythm, the instructor should teach the students to walk each of these basic steps using the proper position, leading, following, and style. After the students have the ability to walk rhythmically through each of the basic steps, they should become aware of how dance steps and combinations of steps can be woven together into an attractive dance. The six basic dance steps should be taught initially in 4/4 time at a tempo of approximately 30 bars a minute with each step taking two beats as in the slow steps of the Fox-Trot.

THE WALK STEP

The Walk Step is simply a matter of walking directly forward or backward in a selected ballroom dance position. Initially, beginning dancers should learn to dance walk forward and backward in the Closed Position. Then, they should learn to walk forward in the Semi-Open and Reverse Positions. Lastly, they should learn to walk forward and backward in the Right and Left Side Positions.

THE ROCK STEP

The Rock Step is a spot step wherein the dancers alternately change the weight from one foot to another without moving their feet. The Rock Step can be danced forward, backward, and to either side.

THE CROSS STEP

The Cross Step is a popular dance step performed by crossing the free foot in front of or behind the supporting foot. Versions of the Cross Step may require both dancers to cross in front or to cross in back simultaneously; some require the man to cross in front while the woman crosses in back; others require the man to cross in back while the woman crosses in front. The Cross Step is an important step to master early because it enables the dancers to move in and out of several dance positions, notably the Closed, Semi-Open, Reverse, Right Side and Left Side Positions.

Walk Step   Rock Step   Cross Step

THE PIVOT STEP

The Pivot Step is performed by rotating on a pivot point that is established by placing the man's right foot inside the woman's right foot. During the Pivot Step, the dancers step with the left foot and keep the right foot in place as it alternately accepts the transfer of weight. The Pivot Step can be danced forward or backward in place, and progressively in a counterclockwise direction by simply moving the right foot in a new pivot point along the line of dance.

THE CHASSÉ STEP

The Chassé Step is danced primarily sideward with one foot stepping to the side and the other closing next to it. If danced forward or backward, the Chassé Step requires that the free foot never pass the supporting foot.

THE HESITATION STEP

The Hesitation Step is one in which the dancers interrupt their movement by holding for at least one count. This is generally done by touching the free foot to the side of the heel of the supporting foot without a transfer of weight. It can also be performed by dotting, drawing and swinging the free foot during the hold.

In summary, the six Basic Ballroom Dance Steps are the foundation for dance patterns and combinations of patterns. Students should learn to move smoothly and accurately from one basic dance step to another in 4/4 time with each step taking two beats. Instructors may wish to pick up the tempo later by asking the students to perform these steps at a tempo of one step per beat. Having learned the basic steps, the students are prepared to receive instruction in the proper rhythm, tempo and style of each ballroom dance form.

Pivot Step

Chassé Step

Hesitation Step

BALLROOM DANCE TERMS

The following abbreviations will appear throughout this text, primarily in the descriptions of the dance steps. The list of definitions should aid the learner in understanding the language of ballroom dance.

ABBREVIATIONS:

ALOD	Against Line of Dance	M	Man
		Meas	Measure
A	Arch	O	Open
Bwd	Backward	Pv	Pivot
BwdX	Backward Cross	Pt	Point
Bal	Balance	Pos	Position
Br	Break	q	Quick
Ch	Change	Rev	Reverse
Cw	Clockwise	RLOD	Reverse Line of Dance
Cl	Closed		
Ct	Count	RH	Right Hand
Ccw	Counterclockwise	RTn	Right Turn
X	Cross	Rk	Rock
Diag	Diagonal	SO	Semi-Open
Dr	Draw	Sd	Side
Ft	Foot	Sk	Skaters
Fwd	Forward	S	Slow
FwdX	Forward Cross	St	Step
FO	Full Open	Sw	Swing
Ho	Hold	Tg	Together
Hp	Hop	Tc	Touch
IP	In Place	Tr	Transfer
K	Kick	Tn	Turn
L	Left	2 H	Two Hand
LH	Left Hand	Wt	Weight
LTn	Left Turn	W	Woman
LOD	Line of Dance	Wp	Wrap

DEFINITIONS

Against Line of Dance—Movement clockwise around the dance floor.

Arch—Partners join and raise hands so that one or both dancers can dance under the raised arms.

Balance—Step left (or right), touch right (or left), and hold. Steps can be taken forward, backward, or to the side.

Ball change—Two weight changes on the ball of the same foot.

Brush—Brush the floor with moving foot as it passes the supporting foot.

Chassé—A side, close, side step pattern with the free foot never passing the supporting foot.

Close—Bring the feet together and transfer weight.

Contrabody movement—A styling movement involving opposite movement of body parts to create a more graceful body line.

Corté (Dip)—A backward step taking full weight by bending the supporting knee. The free leg remains extended with the toe contacting the floor. The Corté can also be done by stepping forward.

Cross—A movement where one foot is crossed in front or in back of the other foot.

Dig—Touching free foot behind supporting foot with strong emphasis.

Dip—See *Corté*.

Dot—Touch toe of free foot behind supporting foot.

Draw—A sideward step that brings the free foot to a closed position without changing weight.

Flare—A style of step in which the free leg swings in an arc-like movement around the pivoting, supporting foot.

Heel Pivot—A turn on the heel of one foot during which no change of weight occurs.

Heel Turn—A turn on the heel of the stepping foot, with the closing foot kept parallel to it throughout the turn and accepting the weight at the conclusion of the turn.

Hesitation—A balance step held for at least one count.

Hop—A transfer of weight, by a springing action, from one foot to another.

In Place—A shift of weight without any directional movement.

Kick—A quick foot movement forward, backward, or sideward without a transfer of weight.

Lead—The cue given by the hand, arm or body to indicate the beginning and end of a movement.

Line of Dance—The counterclockwise, circular direction of dancers around the dance floor.

Measure—A grouping of musical beats made by the regular occurrence of heavy beat.

Meter—Refers to time in music or grouping of beats to form the underlying rhythm within a measure.

Pivot—A turn made in either direction on the ball of the foot.

Point—Pointing toe of free foot in specified direction.

Quick—A quick step takes half the length of time as a slow step and is usually done in pairs.

Reverse Line of Dance—The clockwise, circular movement of dancers around the dance floor.

Rise and Fall—The undulating movement of the body while dancing.

Rock—A movement transferring weight back and forth without changing foot positions.

Routine—One or more steps in a set pattern.

Slow—A slow step equals the length of time of two quick steps.

Sway—The inclining of the body to the right or left, particularly on turns.

Swivel—A twisting motion of the lower body performed on the balls of the feet.

Touch—A foot movement where the feet are brought together without a transfer of weight.

Transfer—A return of weight to free foot after a step.

Varsouvienne—A dance position in which the dancers assume a side-by-side position, facing the same direction with hands joined in a raised position; also called Sweetheart Position.

Vine—A four-step pattern: side, backward cross, side, forward cross.

Visual Cue—A method of leading in free position in which any change in the man's dance step is observed and repeated by the woman as her next dance step.

Wheel—A spot turn performed generally in the Right or Left Side Dance Position.

Weight Change—A transfer of weight from one foot to another.

some fundamentals of music

To a great extent, good dance instruction rests on a knowledge of the fundamentals of music theory which enables the instructor to go beyond the physical act of simply moving to music. Good dancers not only hear the music; they feel it and respond expressively to it. It is essential, therefore, that the teacher introduce each course with the fundamentals of music.

NOTATION

Musical notation consists of symbols that represent the sounds and silences of music. The musical sounds are called *tones*. Tones have four basic characteristics: pitch, duration, intensity, and timbre. Pitch is the relative highness and lowness of tones. Duration is the relative longness or shortness of tones. Intensity is the relative loudness or softness of tones. And, timbre is the tone quality that enables the listener to distinguish between tones produced by different instruments.

In musical notation the symbol used to express pitch and duration of sounds (tones) is the *note*, whereas the symbol used to express silences in music is the *rest*. Notes and rests have a definite durational value although the duration of similar notes or rests may vary from one melody to another simply because they are played at different tempos. The most frequently used notes and rests are the following:

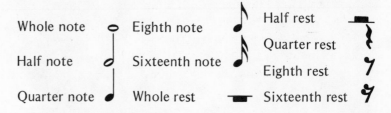

Whole note		Eighth note		Half rest	
Half note		Sixteenth note		Quarter rest	
				Eighth rest	
Quarter note		Whole rest		Sixteenth rest	

The duration of a half note is one-half as long as a whole note, while the duration of a quarter note is one-fourth of a whole note. Similarly, it takes eight eighth notes and sixteen sixteenth notes to equal a whole note. The duration values of rests correspond to their equivalent note values.

Another symbol that indicates a duration of tone is the *dot* (·). A dot placed after a note increases the note's value one-half. For example, a dot after a half note (♩) increases its value to the equivalent of three quarter notes (♩♩♩). What must be understood is that the exact duration of a note is determined by the tempo of the melody. In a fast tempo, a note is of shorter duration than the same note in a slow tempo. Once the musician establishes the tempo of the melody, he or she must follow the relative durational value of each note.

Musical notation is placed on a staff consisting of five lines with four intervening spaces. Music is usually divided on the staff into parts called *measures* by vertical lines called *bar lines*. The upper staff is called the *treble (G) staff* and the lower staff is called the *bass (F) staff*. The two-staff arrangement is called the *grand staff*.

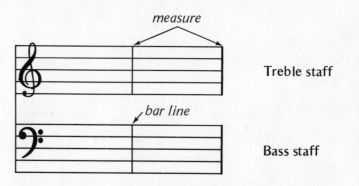

GRAND STAFF

The pitch of a note is indicated by its placment on a staff. The higher its placement, the higher its tone. The pitch of a note may be raised a half tone by placing a sharp (#) before the note, and the pitch may be lowered a half tone by placing a flat (♭) before the note. In musical notation sharps and flats may be cancelled by a natural sign (♮) which, in essence, restores the original pitch of a

18

note when placed before it. Sharps, flats, and naturals are called *accidentals* in musical notation.

The musical alphabet consists of A, B, C, D, E, F, and G. It is used to identify the consecutive pitch names of notes as indicated in the grand staff below:

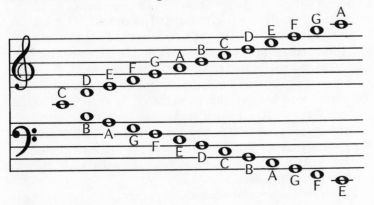

Middle C, which is the C nearest the center of a piano keyboard, appears on a ledger line between the treble and bass staffs. Additional ledger lines may be used to extend the range of a staff as shown above.

RHYTHM AND METER

Rhythm is the motion of music through time. As music moves through time, regular pulsations called *beats* occur. All beats are of equal duration and occur in a continous pattern of strong and weak beats. The organization of beats into musical patterns is called *meter*.

The number of beats of music may vary in a metric pattern. However, all metric patterns will have a strong first beat and a weak last beat. The simplest metric pattern is the *duple* which contains one strong beat followed by a weak beat. A metric pattern with three beats is called *triple meter*. It has a strong beat followed by two weaker beats. *Quadruple meter* is a four-beat pattern which is a combination of two duple meters. The first and third beats are strong while the second and fourth are weak. Frequently, metric patterns that have more than four beats also occur in music. These patterns are developed by combining duples and triples in various ways.

In a metric pattern, the unit of beat is represented by a note of definite durational value. The exact duration of a beat is determined, however, by the tempo of the music. Once the unit of beat is established, it remains the same throughout a given metric pattern.

There are two beat types, simple and compound. Simple beats are those that can be divided equally into twos, while compound beats can be divided equally into threes.

19

Metric pattern, unit of beat, and beat types are expressed in music notation by two numbers known as the *meter signature*, or *time signature*. These numbers appear at the beginning of a piece of music and wherever the meter changes. The top number in time signatures that involve a simple beat type indicates the number of beats in a measure, or the metric pattern. The bottom number in these signatures indicates the unit of beat. For example, a 3/4 time signature means that there are three beats in a measure with each quarter note receiving one beat.

In time signatures involving a compound beat type, the top number, which is always divisible by three, indicates the number of divisions in the entire metric pattern; the bottom number indicates the unit of beat. For example, the time signature 9/8 means that there are nine divisions in the metric pattern of each measure with each eighth note receiving one beat.

In both simple and compound meter, the top number is the most important to the dancer for it indicates the metric pattern of the melody. Melodies written in 3/4, 3/8, and 3/2 time are simple meters common in Waltzes, while 9/8 time is a compound meter also used for the triple metric pattern of the Waltz. Melodies written in 2/4 and 4/4 time are simple meters, and 6/4 and 6/8 are compound meters common to ballroom dance forms other than the Waltz.

TIME SIGNATURES

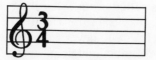

Three beats per measure

Quarter note receives one count

Two beats per measure

Quarter note receives one count

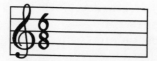

Six beats per measure

Eighth note receives one count

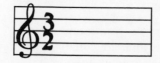

Three beats per measure

Half note receives one count

The most important verbal skill in dance instruction is cuing. The ability to give precise and timely cues rests principally on the teacher, who communicates to the students by counting aloud the beats of the music. The illustration below shows the ways to count music in which the quarter note is the unit of beat and receives one count.

During the initial lesson of each ballroom dance form, the instructor must explain the unique rhythm and meter of its music. By simply playing the music, the instructor should be able to clearly indicate the metric and accent patterns of a melody.

The typical popular melody consists of four periods, eight measures in length, for a total of thirty-two measures. Each period is usually subdivided into phrases two or four measures in length. These phrases, notated by a curved line above or below a group of notes, are complete musical passages that express a particular mood of the melody. As dancers become more proficient, they will become increasingly aware of musical composition and will respond to the accent and dynamic quality of a melody with expressive dance patterns.

The phrases of four melodies are given below. They clearly illustrate the metric pattern of their respective melodies and exemplify the completeness and accent of phrases.

4

the fox-trot

Popularized during the Roaring Twenties, the Fox-Trot has become America's fundamental ballroom dance form. Since 1913 when it was introduced by Harry Fox, a musical comedy star of the Ziegfield show, the Fox-Trot has evolved from a trotting dance that typified the lively post-World War I era into a smooth and graceful ballroom dance.

Because most music today is writtin in 4/4 time, the Fox-Trot serves as a basic dance form for all dance enthusiasts. Once the basic Fox-Trot rhythm is learned, one can move respondingly to other ballroom dances as well as the present-day free and uninhibited fad dances.

TEMPO

Fox-Trot tempo may range from very slow to fast. However, most dancers, particularly beginners, favor music played at 120 to 140 beats per minute.

RHYTHM

The Fox-Trot is danced to music written in 4/4 time with the first and third beats of each measure more heavily accented. It is danced in several combinations of slow and quick steps, with each slow step taking two beats and each quick step one beat of music. Therefore, a dance step in slow, quick, quick (Sqq) rhythm takes one measure of 4/4 time, while a dance step in slow, slow, quick, quick (SSqq) rhythm takes one and a half measures.

The beginner's section of the Fox-Trot includes only steps in the basic rhythm—slow, slow, quick, quick. The advanced section includes additional steps written primarily in slow, quick, quick rhythm; slow, slow, slow, quick quick rhythm; and slow, slow, quick, quick, quick, quick rhythm.

The music notation for the Fox-Trot is as follows:

	SSqq Rhythm				*Sqq Rhythm*	
4/4	♩♩♩♩	♩♩ ♩	♩♩♩♩ ‖		♩♩♩♩ ♩ ♩♩ ‖	
Count	1 2 3 4	1 2 3-4	1 2 3 4		1 2 3 4	1-2 3 4
Rhythm	S S	q q S	S q q		S q q	S q q

	SSSqq Rhythm			
4/4	♩♩♩♩	♩ ♩♩	♩ ♩♩	♩♩♩♩ ‖
Count	1 2 3 4	1-2 3 4	1-2 3 4	1 2 3 4
Rhythm	S S	S q q	S S	S q q

	SSqqqq Rhythm			
4/4	♩♩♩♩	♩♩♩♩	♩ ♩	♩♩♩♩ ‖
Count	1 2 3 4	1 2 3 4	1-2 3-4	1 2 3 4
Rhythm	S S	q q q q	S S	q q q q

STEPS

The steps included in the Fox-Trot are the following:

Beginner's Section: SSqq Rhythm—Fox-Trot Basic, Left Turn, Right Turn, Cross, Semi-Open Walk, Swing Cross, Rock, Arch, Wheel, Pivot, Ball Turn, Hesitation, Sweetheart, and Dip

Advanced Section: SSqq Rhythm—Fox-Trot Basic, Travel, Left Turn, Right Turn, Crossover, Back Cross, Weave, and Break

SSSqq Rhythm—Fox-Trot Basic, Travel, Progressive Left Turn, Progressive Right Turn, and Wheel

SSqqqq Rhythm—Advanced Left Turn, Right Turn, and Advanced Pivot

STYLING

The basic ballroom dance posture as described in chapter 2 is used for the Fox-Trot. The dancers should stand erect with hips forward and in contact with each other at the waist. Their movement should be smooth and graceful, characterized by combinations of long, reaching, slow steps and lively, quick steps that enable them to travel throughout the ballroom floor. As the tempo of the music increases, they should take shorter steps in order to dance with ease, correctness, and expression without succumbing to a carefree interpretation of a faster rhythm.

The use of sway and rise and fall to achieve proper styling in the Fox-Trot is frequently overdone by beginning dancers. The teacher should emphasize initially a smooth initiation and conclusion of each step and then a flowing transition from one dance step to another. Once the dancers learn to move smoothly using the basic steps, the teacher should point out the subtleties of sway and rise and fall already acquired in their dancing. Essentially, sway in the Fox-Trot occurs in the direction of all turns and in the direction of side-close steps. For example, the woman should sway to the man's right on right turns and to his left on side-close steps in SSqq rhythm. Generally, the dancers will rise slightly on the first quick step and fall at the end of the last quick step of a dance rhythm.

TEACHING THE FOX-TROT

Surveys of dance classes frequently reveal that the Fox-Trot receives low ratings as compared to the popularity of other ballroom dances. The primary reasons given for the low rating are that the dancing style is too formal and that the music is too slow and out of date. Unfortunately, too many teachers relax their emphasis on style and select popular rock-type music that lacks the tempo and beat of the Fox-Trot. Teachers must remember that each ballroom dance has its own style, which is learned most readily when danced to music written specifically for it.

Since the Fox-Trot is a traveling dance, the instructor must organize the class so that the dancers move in the same direction during the instructional and free dance periods. During the initial lessons, the couples should be arranged so that they can dance back and forth across the dance floor as the instructor cues the dance steps. After the students have learned a few steps, the instructor should develop some easy routines that move the dancers about the floor in an assigned space. Finally, the instructor should challenge the students to create their own routines and to dance freely in line of dance (LOD) about the dance floor.

It is advisable to begin teaching the Fox-Trot by directing students to walk to the music in Open Position by first taking one step per beat and then one step for every two beats of music. In this way, the students are given the feeling of rhythm changes. After the dancers have learned to walk in slow and quick steps in the Open Position, the instructor should have them walk in Semi-Open, Closed, and Right and Left Side Positions. Mastery of the Walk (see chapter 2) is a prerequisite to learning Fox-Trot steps that require changes of rhythm. Good dancers can walk beautifully in and out of dance positions, creating a very attractive dance particularly to music with a very slow tempo.

Throughout instruction the teacher must give rhythmic, foot and directional cues that are timely and clear. As the students learn the dance steps, the teacher should combine the cues in order to assist students with different problems. For example, the cue "Left, Right, Quick, Quick," will correct students who are using the wrong foot and are out of rhythm, whereas the cue "Slow, Slow, Side, Close" will correct students who are out of rhythm and stepping in the wrong direction. Cuing in this manner enables the instructor to teach the class, and at the same time, to assist the individual who has difficulty with a step. After the class has learned several steps, the teacher may begin cuing by the name of the dance step, such as "Fox-Trot Basic, Left Turn, Left Turn, Fox-Trot Basic." One cannot over-emphasize the importance of precise cuing in ballroom dance. Therefore, teachers should rehearse their cues in order to gain efficient control of their classes.

BEGINNING SECTION

FOX-TROT BASIC

Position—Closed

Man's Part

	Foot	Rhythm	Direction	Lead
1.	L	S	Fwd	Body
2.	R	S	Fwd	
3.	L	q	Sd	Palm
4.	R	q	Cl	

Woman's Part

	Foot	Rhythm	Direction
1.	R	S	Bwd
2.	L	S	Bwd
3.	R	q	Sd
4.	L	q	Cl

Teaching Hints

The Fox-Trot Basic is also danced in a backward direction with the man leading into this step with a palm lead. Remember to reach with the toe pointing downward on the forward and backward steps.

LEFT TURN

Position—Closed

Man's Part

	Foot	Rhythm	Direction	Lead
1.	L	S	Fwd	Body
2.	R	S	Bwd (LTn)	Fingertips
3.	L	q	Sd	
4.	R	q	Cl	

Woman's Part

	Foot	Rhythm	Direction
1.	R	S	Bwd
2.	L	S	Fwd (LTn)
3.	R	q	Sd
4.	L	q	Cl

Teaching Hints

The dancers should look to their lefts as they turn. The man should avoid the tendency to lower his left hand during this turn, which can inhibit an attractive sway to the left on steps 2 and 3.

RIGHT TURN

Position—Closed

Man's Part

	Foot	Rhythm	Direction	Lead
1.	L	S	Bwd	RH Palm
2.	R	S	Fwd (RTn)	RH Heel
3.	L	q	Sd	
4.	R	q	Cl	

Woman's Part

	Foot	Rhythm	Direction
1.	R	S	Fwd
2.	L	S	Bwd (RTn)
3.	R	q	Sd
4.	L	q	Cl

Teaching Hints

The dancers should look to the right as they turn. The man must keep his right elbows raised to ensure a smooth sway on steps 2 and 3.

CROSS

Position—Closed to Semi-Open

Man's Part

	Foot	Rhythm	Direction	Lead
1.	L	S	Fwd	Body
2.	R	S	Bwd	
3.	L	q	Sd	RH Heel
4.	R	q	Fwd X	

Woman's Part

	Foot	Rhythm	Direction
1.	R	S	Bwd
2.	L	S	Fwd
3.	R	q	Sd
4.	L	q	Fwd X

Teaching Hints

The Cross Step concludes with the dancers in Semi-Open Position and leads smoothly into the Semi-Open Walk. Once this step is mastered, a variation should be learned where the dancers conclude the Cross Step in the Closed Position by simply turning toward each other at the end of the fourth step.

SEMI-OPEN WALK

Position—Semi-Open to Closed

Man's Part

	Foot	Rhythm	Direction	Lead
1.	L	S	Fwd	RH Palm
2.	R	S	Fwd	
3.	L	q	Sd (RTn)	RH Fingertips
4.	R	q	Cl	

Woman's Part

	Foot	Rhythm	Direction
1.	R	S	Fwd
2.	L	S	Fwd
3.	R	q	Sd (LTn)
4.	L	q	Cl

Teaching Hints

An excellent variation to the Semi-Open Walk can be added on the third step. Instead of turning right on the third step to face his partner, the man should continue dancing forward while the woman turns 180° to a Closed Position. Also, this step may be danced for several measures in the Semi-Open or Open Positions before returning to the Closed Position.

SWING CROSS

Position—Closed to Right Side

Man's Part

	Foot	Rhythm	Direction	Lead
1.	L	S	Sd	RH Palm
2.	R	S	Sd	
3.	L	q	Sd	RH Fingertips
4.	R	q	Fwd X	

Woman's Part

	Foot	Rhythm	Direction
1.	R	S	Sd
2.	L	S	Sd
3.	R	q	Sd
4.	L	q	Bwd X

Teaching Hints

This step is used frequently in teaching students to move smoothly into a Right Side Position. A variation of this step (Sd,Sd,Sd,BX) is used to dance smoothly from the Closed to the Left Side Position. The man may lead out of Side Position by dancing two steps (S,S) in a Side Position and then returning to the Closed Position on the quick steps.

ROCK

Forward Rock Position—Closed

Man's Part

	Foot	Rhythm	Direction	Lead
1.	L	S	Fwd	Body
2.	R	S	IP	RH Palm
3.	L	q	Sd	
4.	R	q	Cl	

Woman's Part

	Foot	Rhythm	Direction
1.	R	S	Bwd
2.	L	S	IP
3.	R	q	Sd
4.	L	q	Cl

Backward Rock Position—Closed

Man's Part

	Foot	Rhythm	Direction	Lead
1.	L	S	Bwd	RH Palm
2.	R	S	IP	Body
3.	L	q	Sd	
4.	R	q	Cl	

Woman's Part

	Foot	Rhythm	Direction
1.	R	S	Fwd
2.	L	S	IP
3.	R	q	Sd
4.	L	q	Cl

Side Rock Position—Closed

Man's Part

	Foot	Rhythm	Direction	Lead
1.	L	S	Sd	RH Palm
2.	R	S	IP	
3.	L	q	Sd	
4.	R	q	Cl	

Woman's Part

	Foot	Rhythm	Direction
1.	R	S	Sd
2.	L	S	IP
3.	R	q	Sd
4.	L	q	Cl

Teaching Hints

Rock steps should be performed with reaching forward and backward steps to assure good posture and styling. These steps are used frequently on crowded dance floors.

ARCH

Position—Closed to Arch to Semi-Open

Man's Part

	Foot	Rhythm	Direction	Lead
1.	L	S	Fwd (LTn)	LH High
2.	R	S	Fwd	RH Palm
3.	L	q	Fwd	
4.	R	q	Fwd	

Woman's Part

	Foot	Rhythm	Direction
1.	R	S	Fwd (RTn)
2.	L	S	Fwd (RPv)
3.	R	q	Bwd (RTn)
4.	L	q	Fwd

Teaching Hints

A strong lead that combines a raised left hand and right palm pressure assures the dancers of forward movement on steps 1 and 2. This step can lose its attractiveness if the man stops his forward movement instead of dancing down the line of dance as the woman turns in place.

WHEEL

Position—Right Side

Man's Part

	Foot	Rhythm	Direction	Lead
1.	L	S	Fwd	RH palm
2.	R	S	Fwd	
3.	L	q	Fwd	
4.	R	q	Fwd	

Woman's Part

	Foot	Rhythm	Direction
1.	R	S	Fwd
2.	L	S	Fwd
3.	R	q	Fwd
4.	L	q	Fwd

Teaching Hints

In this step, a fingertip lead is required to move from the Closed to Right Side Position, whereas a heel lead is given for dancing from a Right Side to a Closed Position. Movement in and out of these dance positions occurs on the quick steps. During the Wheel Step the dancers should look at each other.

PIVOT

Position—Closed

Man's Part

	Foot	Rhythm	Direction	Lead
1.	L	S	Bwd	RH Palm
2.	R	S	Fwd (RPv)	Body
3.	L	q	Bwd	RH Palm
4.	R	q	Fwd (RPv)	Body

Woman's Part

	Foot	Rhythm	Direction
1.	R	S	Fwd (RPv)
2.	L	S	Bwd
3.	R	q	Fwd (RPv)
4.	L	q	Bwd

Teaching Hints

The Pivot Step requires a definite feeling of contra-body movement. Dancers can achieve this by placing the inside of their pivoting right feet together and pushing off their left feet.

BALL TURN

Position—Closed to Right Side

Man's Part

	Foot	Rhythm	Direction	Lead
1.	L	S	Sd	RH Palm
2.	R	S	Fwd X (LPv)	RH Heel
3.	L	q	IP	
4.	R	q	IP	

Woman's Part

	Foot	Rhythm	Direction
1.	R	S	Sd
2.	L	S	Fwd X (LPv)
3.	R	q	Fwd
4.	L	q	Bwd

Teaching Hints

In effect, this is only a two-step pattern for the man who turns 180° with a pivot in place on both feet in steps 3 and 4. There is a pronounced sway to the left, a rise at the start of the pivot, and a fall at the end of the pivot. (See photograph.)

HESITATION

Position—Closed

Man's Part

	Foot	Rhythm	Direction	Lead
1.	L	S	Sd	RH Palm
2.	R	S	Pt	
3.	R	q	Cl	
4.	L	q	IP	
5.	R	S	Sd	RH Palm
6.	L	S	Pt	
7.	L	q	Cl	
8.	R	q	IP	

Woman's Part

	Foot	Rhythm	Direction
1.	R	S	Sd
2.	L	S	Pt
3.	L	q	Cl
4.	R	q	IP
5.	L	S	Sd
6.	R	S	Pt
7.	R	q	Cl
8.	L	q	IP

Ball Turn

32

Teaching Hints

The Hesitation is performed in several ways: by pointing to the side with the non-supporting foot; by dotting behind the supporting foot; and by touching beside the supporting foot.

SWEETHEART

Position—Closed to Sweetheart to Closed

Man's Part

	Foot	Rhythm	Direction	Lead
1.	L	S	BwdX	LH High
2.	R	S	Bwd (LTn)	
3.	L	q	Bwd	
4.	R	q	Bwd	
5.	L	S	Fwd	LH High
6.	R	S	Fwd	
7.	L	q	Fwd	
8.	R	q	Fwd	

Woman's Part

	Foot	Rhythm	Direction
1.	R	S	FwdX
2.	L	S	Bwd (LTn)
3.	R	q	Bwd
4.	L	q	Bwd
5.	R	S	Fwd
6.	L	S	Bwd (RTn)
7.	R	q	Bwd
8.	L	q	Bwd

Sweetheart

Teaching Hints

Essentially, this step entails moving in and out of a right-side Sweetheart Position. If they wish, dancers may do several Travel Steps in the Sweetheart Position before returning to the Closed Position. The left-hand lead is primarily a pulling motion that turns the woman in and out of the two dance positions. (See photographs.)

Sweetheart

DIP

Position—Closed

Man's Part

	Foot	Rhythm	Direction	Lead
1.	L	S	Sd (Dip)	Palm
2.	L	S	Ho (Dip)	Body
3.	R	q	IP	
4.	L	q	Tc	

Dip

Woman's Part

	Foot	Rhythm	Direction
1.	R	S	Sd (Dip)
2.	R	S	Ho (Dip)
3.	L	q	Sd
4.	R	q	Tc

Teaching Hints

This step is used frequently to conclude a dance, however, it also can be used effectively throughout a dance routine. Initially, beginners may lose their balance if the man fails to keep his back upright while holding his partner over his flexed, supporting left knee. The woman supports some of her weight on her right foot while pointing her left toe to the floor. Correctly performed, the Dip is a deep, lasting sway to the man's left. (See photograph.)

BEGINNING ROUTINES

The following routines are designed to move the couples back and forth across the ballroom floor.

ROUTINE ONE

1. Fox-Trot Basic
2. Fox-Trot Basic
3. Cross
4. Semi-Open Walk
5. Left Turn
6. Left Turn
7. Repeat in reverse direction

ROUTINE TWO

1. Fox-Trot Basic
2. Fox-Trot Basic
3. Forward Rock
4. Arch
5. Fox-Trot Basic
6. Right Turn
7. Right Turn
8. Repeat in reverse direction

ROUTINE THREE

1. Fox-Trot Basic
2. Fox-Trot Basic
3. Wheel (180°)
4. Wheel (180°)
5. Fox-Trot Basic
6. Pivot
7. Repeat in reverse direction

ROUTINE FOUR

1. Hesitation
2. Fox-Trot Basic
3. Fox-Trot Basic
4. Dip
5. Fox-Trot Basic
6. Ball Turn
7. Fox-Trot Basic (Right Side to Closed Position)
8. Repeat in reverse direction

ADVANCED SECTION

This section includes steps written in three rhythms—Sqq, SSSqq, and SSqqqq. Mastery of these rhythms of the Fox-Trot will give balance to dance combinations by requiring the dancers to begin dance steps on either the right or the left foot. However, Arthur Murray's magic rhythm (SSqq) still remains the foundation upon which the good dancer builds a repertoire of steps in various rhythms.

Changing dance rhythms can be learned quickly and danced smoothly if the dancers retain good dancing position throughout each step. The leads must be precise, and in effect, they must become part of a total body lead that enables the dancers to move as one.

Fox-Trot—Sqq Rhythm

BASIC STEP

Position—Closed

Man's Part

	Foot	Rhythm	Direction	Lead
1.	L	S	Fwd	Body
2.	R	q	Sd	RH Palm
3.	L	q	Cl	
4.	R	S	Bwd	RH Palm
5.	L	q	Sd	
6.	R	q	Cl	

Woman's Part

	Foot	Rhythm	Direction
1.	R	S	Bwd
2.	L	q	Sd
3.	R	q	Cl
4.	L	S	Fwd
5.	R	q	Sd
6.	L	q	Cl

Teaching Hints

The palm lead that checks the woman's backward movement on the second step must be timely or she may continue dancing backward in SSqq rhythm.

TRAVEL

Position—Closed

Man's Part

	Foot	Rhythm	Direction	Lead
1.	L	S	Fwd	Body
2.	R	q	Sd	RH Palm
3.	L	q	Cl	
4.	R	S	Fwd	Body
5.	L	q	Sd	RH Palm
6.	R	q	Cl	

Woman's Part

	Foot	Rhythm	Direction
1.	R	S	Bwd
2.	L	q	Sd
3.	R	q	Cl
4..	L	S	Bwd
5.	R	q	Sd
6.	L	q	Cl

Teaching Hints

Although this step is not used frequently, it is an important step because it requires the students to begin dance steps with either foot. In the Fox-Trot rhythm (SSqq), the dancers always begin each step with the same foot (man's left, woman's right).

LEFT TURN

Position—Closed

Man's Part

	Foot	Rhythm	Direction	Lead
1.	L	S	Fwd (LTn)	Body
2.	R	q	Sd	
3.	L	q	Cl	
4.	R	S	Bwd (LTn)	RH Fingertips
5.	L	q	Sd	
6.	R	q	Cl	

Woman's Part

	Foot	Rhythm	Direction
1.	R	S	Bwd (LTn)
2.	L	q	Sd
3.	R	q	Cl
4.	L	S	Fwd (LTn)
5.	R	q	Sd
6.	L	q	Cl

Although the turn is initiated on the first step, the turning movement continues through each step. Swaying begins and is pronounced on steps 1 and 4. The couple should look to their lefts during the turn.

RIGHT TURN

Position—Closed

Man's Part

	Foot	Rhythm	Direction	Lead
1.	L	S	Bwd (RTn)	RH Heel
2.	R	q	Sd	
3.	L	q	Cl	
4.	R	S	Fwd (RTn)	Body
5.	L	q	Sd	
6.	R	q	Cl	

Woman's Part

	Foot	Rhythm	Direction
1.	R	S	Fwd (RTn)
2.	L	q	Sd
3.	R	q	Cl
4.	L	S	Bwd (RTn)
5.	R	q	Sd
6.	L	q	Cl

Teaching Hints

Men typically have some trouble with this step because they are turning into their partners. Both partners should learn to turn throughout each step, and the man must remember to keep his right elbow in good position throughout the turn. The couple should look to their right during the turn. Swaying to the right is most pronounced on steps 1 and 4.

CROSSOVER

Position—Closed to Semi-Open to Closed

Man's Part

	Foot	Rhythm	Direction	Lead
1.	L	S	Fwd	Body
2.	R	q	Sd	RH Palm
3.	L	q	Cl	
4.	R	S	FwdX (LTn)	RH Heel
5.	L	q	Sd (RTn)	RH Fingertips
6.	R	q	Cl	

Woman's Part

	Foot	Rhythm	Direction
1.	R	S	Bwd
2.	L	q	Sd
3.	R	q	Cl
4.	L	S	FwdX (RTn)
5.	R	q	Sd (LTn)
6.	L	q	Cl

Teaching Hints

The movement of the Crossover is in a lateral direction since both dancers turn 90° and face each other on step 5. A variation of this step requires the woman to turn 180° into the Closed Position while the man continues forward on step 5.

WEAVE

Position—Reverse to Semi-Open

Weave

Man's Part

	Foot	Rhythm	Direction	Lead
1.	L	S	FwdX	RH Fingertips
2.	R	q	Sd	
3.	L	q	Cl	
4.	R	S	FwdX	RH Heel
5.	L	q	Sd	
6.	R	q	Cl	

Woman's Part

	Foot	Rhythm	Direction
1.	R	S	FwdX
2.	L	q	Sd
3.	R	q	Cl
4.	L	S	FwdX
5.	R	q	Sd
6.	L	q	Cl

Teaching Hints

Some prefer to dance this step in an Open Position where the man alternately places his left and right hands around the waist of his partner while she alternately places her right and left hands at his left and right shoulders respectively. The couple should look in the direction they travel. (See photographs.)

Weave

CROSS

Position—Closed to Semi-Open

Man's Part

	Foot	Rhythm	Direction	Lead
1.	L	S	Fwd	Body
2.	R	q	Sd	RH Palm
3.	L	q	Cl	
4.	R	S	Bwd	RH Palm
5.	L	q	Sd	
6.	R	q	Fwd X	RH Heel

Woman's Part

	Foot	Rhythm	Direction
1.	R	S	Bwd
2.	L	q	Sd
3.	R	q	Cl
4.	L	S	Fwd
5.	R	q	Sd
6.	L	q	Fwd X

Teaching Hints

This step concludes with the dancers in the Semi-Open Position. However, the couple may return to the Closed Position by pivoting and facing each other at the conclusion of step 6.

BREAK

Position—Closed to Open to Closed

Man's Part

	Foot	Rhythm	Direction	Lead
1.	L	S	Sd	RH Palm
2.	R	q	Bwd X	RH Fingertips
3.	L	q	Ip	
4.	R	S	Sd	LH Palm
5.	L	q	Bwd X	LH Fingertips
6.	R	q	IP	

Woman's Part

	Foot	Rhythm	Direction
1.	R	S	Sd
2.	L	q	Bwd X
3.	R	q	IP
4.	L	S	Sd
5.	R	q	Bwd X
6.	L	q	IP

Break

Break

This is essentially a spot step where the couple moves from a left-side to a right-side Open Position. (See photographs.) To return to the Closed Position after this step, the man should check his partner's movement with his right palm and raise his left hand into its normal position.

Fox-Trot SSSqq Rhythm

BASIC STEP

Position—Closed

Man's Part

	Foot	Rhythm	Direction	Lead
1.	L	S	Fwd	Body
2.	R	S	Fwd	
3.	L	S	Fwd	
4.	R	q	Sd	RH Palm
5.	L	q	Cl	
6.	R	S	Bwd	RH Palm
7.	L	S	Bwd	
8.	R	S	Bwd	
9.	L	q	Sd	
10.	R	q	Cl	

Woman's Part

	Foot	Rhythm	Direction
1.	R	S	Bwd
2.	L	S	Bwd
3.	R	S	Bwd
4.	L	q	Sd
5.	R	q	Cl
6.	L	S	Fwd
7.	R	S	Fwd
8.	L	S	Fwd
9.	R	q	Sd
10.	L	q	Cl

Teaching Hints

Although this initially appears to be a simple step, it may be difficult for some to dance in this rhythm. During the forward part, the man must give upper body pressure through the third step, and during the backward portion, he must continue with a strong palm lead.

TRAVEL

Position—Closed

Man's Part

	Foot	Rhythm	Direction	Lead
1.	L	S	Fwd	Body
2.	R	S	Fwd	
3.	L	S	Fwd	
4.	R	q	Sd	RH Palm
5.	L	q	Cl	
6.	R	S	Fwd	Body
7.	L	S	Fwd	
8.	R	S	Fwd	
9.	L	q	Sd	RH Palm
10.	R	q	Cl	

Woman's Part

	Foot	Rhythm	Direction
1.	R	S	Bwd
2.	L	S	Bwd
3.	R	S	Bwd
4.	L	q	Sd
5.	R	q	Cl
6.	L	S	Bwd
7.	R	S	Bwd
8.	L	S	Bwd
9.	R	q	Sd
10.	L	q	Cl

Teaching Hints

The man must continue a strong upper-body lead on the third and eighth steps. Both dancers should take long reaching forward steps.

PROGRESSIVE LEFT TURN

Position—Closed

Man's Part

	Foot	Rhythm	Direction	Lead
1.	L	S	Fwd (LTn)	Body
2.	R	S	Fwd (LTn)	
3.	L	S	Fwd (LTn)	
4.	R	q	Sd	RH Palm
5.	L	q	Cl	
6.	R	S	Bwd (LTn)	RH Palm
7.	L	S	Bwd (LTn)	
8.	R	S	Bwd (LTn)	
9.	L	q	Sd	
10.	R	q	Cl	

Woman's Part

	Foot	Rhythm	Direction
1.	R	S	Bwd (LTn)
2.	L	S	Bwd (LTn)
3.	R	S	Bwd (LTn)
4.	L	q	Sd
5.	R	q	Cl
6.	L	S	Fwd (LTn)
7.	R	S	Fwd (LTn)
8.	L	S	Fwd (LTn)
9.	R	q	Sd
10.	L	q	Cl

Teaching Hints

During the first three steps, the couple dances forward in a counterclockwise direction, and during steps 6, 7, and 8, they dance backward in a counterclockwise direction to achieve a 180° left turn. Very little sway occurs during this step.

PROGRESSIVE RIGHT TURN

Position—Closed

Man's Part

	Foot	Rhythm	Direction	Lead
1.	L	S	Bwd (RTn)	RH Palm
2.	R	S	Bwd (RTn)	
3.	L	S	Bwd (RTn)	
4.	R	q	Sd	
5.	L	q	Cl	
6.	R	S	Fwd (RTn)	Body
7.	L	S	Fwd (RTn)	
8.	R	S	Fwd (RTn)	
9.	L	q	Sd	RH Palm
10.	R	q	Cl	

Woman's Part

	Foot	Rhythm	Direction
1.	R	S	Fwd (RTn)
2.	L	S	Fwd (RTn)
3.	R	S	Fwd (RTn)
4.	L	q	Sd
5.	R	q	Cl
6.	L	S	Bwd (RTn)
7.	R	S	Bwd (RTn)
8.	L	S	Bwd (RTn)
9.	R	q	Sd
10.	L	q	Cl

Teaching Hints

During the first three steps, the couple moves backward in a clockwise direction, and during the sixth, seventh and eighth steps, the couple moves forward in a clockwise direction. Very little sway occurs during this turn.

WHEEL

Position—Right Side

Man's Part

	Foot	Rhythm	Direction	Lead
1.	L	S	Fwd	Body
2.	R	S	Fwd	
3.	L	S	Fwd	
4.	R	q	Fwd	
5.	L	q	Fwd	
6.	R	S	Fwd	
7.	L	S	Fwd	
8.	R	S	Fwd	
9.	L	q	Fwd	
10.	R	q	Fwd	

Woman's Part

	Foot	Rhythm	Direction
1.	R	S	Fwd
2.	L	S	Fwd
3.	R	S	Fwd
4.	L	q	Fwd
5.	R	q	Fwd
6.	L	S	Fwd
7.	R	S	Fwd
8.	L	S	Fwd
9.	R	q	Fwd
10.	L	q	Fwd

Teaching Hints

A fingertip lead moves the couple from Closed to Right Side Position, while a heel lead moves them from Right Side to Closed Position. Movement from one dance position to another occurs during the quick steps. The couple should look at each other while dancing in a Side Position.

Fox-Trot SSqqqq Rhythm

ADVANCED LEFT TURN

Position—Closed

Man's Part

	Foot	Rhythm	Direction	Lead
1.	L	S	Fwd	Body
2.	R	S	Fwd	
3.	L	q	Fwd	
4.	R	q	Bwd (LTn)	RH Fingertips
5.	L	q	Sd	
6.	R	q	Cl	

Woman's Part

	Foot	Rhythm	Direction
1.	R	S	Bwd
2.	L	S	Bwd
3.	R	q	Bwd
4.	L	q	Fwd (LTn)
5.	R	q	Sd
6.	L	q	Cl

Teaching Hints

The four small quick steps enable the couple to turn 180°. To make an attractive turn, the couple must retain a tight Closed Position.

ADVANCED RIGHT TURN

Position—Closed

Man's Part

	Foot	Rhythm	Direction	Lead
1.	L	S	Bwd	RH Palm
2.	R	S	Bwd	
3.	L	q	Bwd	
4.	R	q	Fwd (RTn)	Body & RH Heel
5.	L	q	Sd	
6.	R	q	Cl	

Woman's Part

	Foot	Rhythm	Direction
1.	R	S	Fwd
2.	L	S	Fwd
3.	R	q	Fwd
4.	L	q	Bwd (RTn)
5.	R	q	Sd
6.	L	q	Cl

Teaching Hints

Throughout the four small quick steps, the dancers remain in contact with each other to perform an attractive 180° turn. Without body contact, the step is difficult for the man to perform.

ADVANCED PIVOT

Position—Closed

Man's Part

	Foot	Rhythm	Direction	Lead
1.	L	S	Bwd	Palm
2.	R	S	Fwd (RPv)	Body
3.	L	q	Bwd	Palm
4.	R	q	Fwd (RPv)	Body
5.	L	q	Bwd	Palm
6.	R	q	Fwd (RPv)	Body

Woman's Part

	Foot	Rhythm	Direction
1.	R	S	Fwd (RPv)
2.	L	S	Bwd
3.	R	q	Fwd (RPv)
4.	L	q	Bwd
5.	R	q	Fwd (RPv)
6.	L	q	Bwd

Teaching Hints

As with all clockwise pivot steps, the dancers place the insides of their pivoting right feet together and alternately push off their left feet. The Pivot Step, which requires good contra-body movement, is danced with the couple slightly to the left of the normal Closed Position. The Pivot Step may be continued in any even number of quick steps.

ADVANCED ROUTINES

These routines are choreographed to move the dancers across the ballroom floor.

ROUTINE ONE

1. Fox-Trot Basic (SSSqq)
2. Travel (SSSqq)
3. Progressive Left Turn (180°)
4. Progressive Left Turn (180°)
5. Fox-Trot Basic (Sqq)
6. Left Turn (Sqq)
7. Left Turn (Sqq)
8. Repeat in reverse direction

ROUTINE TWO

1. Travel (Sqq)
2. Travel (Sqq)
3. Back Cross
4. Weave
5. Advanced Left Turn
6. Repeat in reverse direction

ROUTINE THREE

1. Travel (SSSqq)
2. Progressive Right Turn (180°)
3. Progressive Right Turn (180°)
4. Fox-Trot Basic (Sqq)
5. Break
6. Break
7. Fox-Trot Basic
8. Advanced Right Turn
9. Repeat in reverse direction

ROUTINE FOUR

1. Travel (SSSqq)
2. Wheel (180°)
3. Wheel (180°)
4. Advanced Left Turn
5. Advanced Right Turn
6. Advanced Pivot
7. Repeat in reverse direction

5

the swing

It has been said that popular dance is an expression of the mood of the times. Surely in American history this is clearly evidenced in the Lindbergh Hop that was popularized in the exciting, carefree, post-war era described as the Roaring Twenties. The Lindy, as it was later called, is believed to have its origin in the Fox-Trot, a ballroom dance that had emerged just a few years earlier.

Unlike most fad dances, the Lindy has endured the test of time despite the highly expressive and sometimes acrobatic influences of later dances such as the Charleston, the Black Bottom, the Big Apple, the Jitterbug, the Twist, and now the Hustle. Today the Lindy has evolved into the Swing, a smooth yet exuberant ballroom dance characterized by frequent swinging steps.

TEMPO

The tempo for the Swing ranges from fast to very fast. Beginners favor a tempo of 160 to 180 beats per minute while experienced dancers generally enjoy a faster tempo, roughly 180 to 200 beats per minute.

RHYTHM

The Swing is danced to music written in 4/4 time, with the first and third beats of each measure accented but not as heavily as in the Fox-Trot. The dance rhythm of the Swing is a combination of two slow steps and two quick steps. Each slow step takes two beats of music while the quick steps take one beat of music. The Swing, like the

47

Fox-Trot, requires one and one-half measures of music for each dance step written in SSqq rhythm.

The music notation for the Swing is as follows:

SSqq Rhythm

4/4	♩♩♩♩ ♩♩ ♩ ♩ ♩♩ ‖
Count	1 2 3 4 1 2 3-4 1-2 3 4
Rhythm	S S q q S S q q

STEPS

The following steps are presented for the Swing:

Beginner's Section: Rock Basic, Link, Butterfly, Arch, Roll, Spin, Arch and Exchange, Walk By, Wrap and Unwrap, Double Under, and Reverse Spin

Advanced Section: Double Reverse Spin, Double Arch, Wrap Walk, Grapevine, Twister, Sweetheart, Kick, and Touch Walk

STYLING

The Swing enjoys immediate popularity because the fast, bouncy tempo stimulates an atmosphere of exuberance and the styling of the Swing allows for individuality and freedom of expression. Many dancers respond to this invitation for self-expression with delightful spontaneity and unique creativity.

The teacher, while encouraging individuality of style, must stress specific points of style indigenous to the Swing. Throughout the Swing, dancers should retain a rather upright position and refrain from bending too far forward at the waist. Because of the fast tempo the dancers should take short steps with relaxed, flexed knees. This enables them to develop a bouncy, yet smooth, style.

Possibly the most important styling points pertain to the firmness of hand grip and position of arms. Proper hand grip is established as (1) the man extends his hand palm up; (2) the woman places her hand palm down in his hand; and (3) the man tightens his grip by placing his thumb firmly against the woman's fingers. Naturally, as the dancers perform certain steps, the grip must relax to allow for fluid movement.

A firm forearm is necessary to establish a spring-like connection between the dancers so that they can respond to the rapid changes of position characterizing the Swing. Without firm contact, the dancers usually rock away from each other to an unattractive extended arm's length, and consequently, are late for the next step. When dancing in a One-Hand Position, the free arm should be bent at the elbow and move to the beat of the music.

48

The Swing is danced in three distinct foot patterns—Single Lindy (SSqq), Double Lindy (SSqq) and Triple (SSqqSqqS). Since all the steps presented in this text are in SSqq rhythm, only the styling of the Single and Double Lindy will be described.

Most Single and Double Lindy steps are performed in the Link and Semi-Open Positions and danced to a slow, slow, quick, quick rhythm. As a general rule, the man and woman should step toward each other on the slow steps and rock away from each other on the quick steps. The man must use this contra movement as the initiating force to lead his partner from one dance position to another.

The Single Lindy is a distinct four-step pattern (forward, in place, backward, in place) with each step taken in a flat-footed manner. In contrast, the Double Lindy is performed in a touch-step, touch-step, step, step pattern. In the touch-step part of the Double Lindy, both the touch and the step receive one beat of music.

Single Lindy

Man's Part

	Foot	Rhythm	Direction	Style
1.	L	S	Fwd	Step
2.	R	S	IP	Step
3.	L	q	Bwd	Step
4.	R	q	IP	Step

Woman's Part

	Foot	Rhythm	Direction	Style
1.	R	S	Fwd	Step
2.	L	S	IP	Step
3.	R	q	Bwd	Step
4.	L	q	IP	Step

Double Lindy

Man's Part

	Foot	Rhythm	Direction	Style
1.	L	S	Fwd	Touch-Step
2.	R	S	IP	Touch-Step
3.	L	q	Bwd	Step
4.	R	q	IP	Step

Woman's Part

	Foot	Rhythm	Direction	Style
1.	R	S	Fwd	Touch-Step
2.	L	S	IP	Touch-Step
3.	R	q	Bwd	Step
4.	L	q	IP	Step

TEACHING THE SWING

Because of the lively, free movement of this popular dance, students are eager to "swing." Successful teachers capture their enthusiasm and effectively present sequential lessons that allow and encourage a flair for individual style. Unfortunately, some teachers respond to the enthusiasm of their students by introducing new steps too soon rather than following the principle that a few steps danced well are more attractive and enjoyable than many steps danced poorly.

Since the Swing is a spot dance, teachers should arrange their class so that each couple will have a dancing space of at least ten square feet. During the initial lessons, the instructor must remember the difficulties encountered by beginning students attempting to follow the description and demonstration of a new step. Whenever new steps are introduced, it is advisable to organize the class so that the men face the same direction as the male instructor, and the women face the same direction as the female instructor. In this way, it is possible to use the walls of the room as orientative aids, and the students can easily follow the movement of the instructors.

Instruction in the Swing should begin with the Single Lindy because the foot pattern is simpler, and it is easier for the beginner to dance to the beat of the music. Most students, however, favor the style of the Double Lindy because it allows for greater dance expression. Therefore, the Double should be taught as soon as the students master the Single Lindy. Students should learn to dance in both rhythms, using the Single Lindy for the faster tempos and the Double Lindy for the slower tempos.

Throughout the Swing, particularly the spinning and exchanging steps, it is imperative that the instructor give distinct cues. In addition to the rhythmic, foot, and directional cues, more descriptive cues may be included, such as Fwd-Turn-Rock-Fwd for the Arch Step. The most accurate directional cues possible for each step have been used in this book. Nevertheless, in some instances students may find another directional cue more helpful such as Fwd-Bwd-Bwd-Fwd for the Rock Basic instead of Fwd-IP-Bwd-IP.

The Swing steps offered in this text follow two fundamental principles: (1) the man begins each step on the left foot, the woman on the right; and (2) the couple comes together on the slow steps and breaks apart on the quick steps. These points simplify instruction in the Swing and make it possible for dancers to perform some intricate steps and combinations of steps with relative ease.

BEGINNING SECTION

ROCK BASIC

Position—Semi-Open

Man's Part

	Foot	Rhythm	Direction	Lead
1.	L	S	Fwd	RH Palm
2.	R	S	IP	
3.	L	q	Bwd	
4.	R	q	IP	

Woman's Part

	Foot	Rhythm	Direction
1.	R	S	Fwd
2.	L	S	IP
3.	R	q	Bwd
4.	L	q	IP

Teaching Hints

Although this step has a very simple pattern, it is an attractive step if performed properly. During the forward part of the step, the dancers should turn in a near cheek-to-cheek position, whereas, in the backward part, they should break away slightly from each other. (See photograph.)

LINK

Position—One or Two Hand

Rock Basic

Man's Part

	Foot	Rhythm	Direction	Lead
1.	L	S	Fwd	Pull
2.	R	S	IP	
3.	L	q	Bwd	Push
4.	R	q	IP	

Woman's Part

	Foot	Rhythm	Direction
1.	R	S	Fwd
2.	L	S	IP
3.	R	q	Bwd
4.	L	q	IP

Teaching Hints

This is a basic step that characterizes the Swing and "links" other steps into attractive routines. The Link Step can be performed in any combination of One-Hand or Two-Hand Positions such as man's left and woman's right, man's right and woman's right, or two-hands crossed. The lead is a *pull* that brings the couple together and a *push* that rocks them apart.

BUTTERFLY

Position—Two Hand

Man's Part

	Foot	Rhythm	Direction	Lead
1.	L	S	Fwd	Pull
2.	R	S	Bwd X	Push
3.	L	q	Bwd	
4.	R	q	IP	

Woman's Part

	Foot	Rhythm	Direction
1.	R	S	Fwd X
2.	L	S	Bwd
3.	R	q	Bwd
4.	L	q	IP

Teaching Hints

Essentially this is a turning Link Step. In the forward part of this step, the dancers should step to each other's right side so that their right shoulders almost touch. To perform this step smoothly, the dancers pull and push each other in and out of this step. (See photograph.)

Butterfly

ARCH

Arch In

Position—One Hand (L to R) to Semi-Open

Man's Part

	Foot	Rhythm	Direction	Lead
1.	L	S	Fwd	LH High
2.	R	S	IP	
3.	L	q	Bwd	
4.	R	q	IP	

Woman's Part

	Foot	Rhythm	Direction
1.	R	S	Fwd (LTn)
2.	L	S	Bwd
3.	R	q	Bwd
4.	L	q	IP

Arch Out

Position—Semi-Open to One Hand (L to R)

Man's Part

	Foot	Rhythm	Direction	Lead
1.	L	S	Fwd	LH High
2.	R	S	IP	
3.	L	q	Bwd	
4.	R	q	IP	

Woman's Part

	Foot	Rhythm	Direction
1.	R	S	Fwd (RTn)
2.	L	S	Bwd
3.	R	q	Bwd
4.	L	q	IP

Teaching Hints

During the Arch the man simply performs the basic step while the woman turns under the arch. The left-hand lead of the man entails raising the joined hands and pulling the woman in or out of the Semi-Open Position. (See photograph of Arch Position in chapter 2.)

ROLL

Roll In
Position—One Hand (R to R) to Skaters

Man's Part

	Foot	Rhythm	Direction	Lead
1.	L	S	Fwd	RH Pull
2.	R	S	IP	
3.	L	q	Bwd	
4.	R	q	IP	

Woman's Part

	Foot	Rhythm	Direction
1.	R	S	Fwd (LTn)
2.	L	S	Bwd
3.	R	q	Bwd
4.	L	q	IP

Roll Out
Position—Skaters to One Hand (R to R)

Man's Part

	Foot	Rhythm	Direction	Lead
1.	L	S	Fwd	RH Push
2.	R	S	IP	
3.	L	q	Bwd	
4.	R	q	IP	

Woman's Part

	Foot	Rhythm	Direction
1.	R	S	Fwd (RTn)
2.	L	S	Bwd
3.	R	q	Bwd
4.	L	q	IP

Teaching Hints

The footwork of this step is identical to the Arch. The lead for the Roll In is a right-hand pull that turns the woman counterclockwise into the Skaters Position. Right-hand pressure against the woman's right side rolls her out of the Skaters Position. Dancers may also roll in and out of the Sweetheart Position.

SPIN

Spin In

Position—One Hand (L to R) to Semi-Open

Man's Part

	Foot	Rhythm	Direction	Lead
1.	L	S	Fwd	LH Pull
2.	R	S	IP	
3.	L	q	Bwd	
4.	R	q	IP	

Woman's Part

	Foot	Rhythm	Direction
1.	R	S	Fwd (LTn)
2.	L	S	Bwd
3.	R	q	Bwd
4.	L	q	IP

Spin Out

Position—Semi-Open to One Hand (L to R)

Man's Part

	Foot	Rhythm	Direction	Lead
1.	L	S	Fwd	RH Push
2.	R	S	IP	
3.	L	q	Bwd	
4.	R	q	IP	

Woman's Part

	Foot	Rhythm	Direction
1.	R	S	Fwd (RTn)
2.	L	S	Bwd
3.	R	q	Bwd
4.	L	q	IP

Teaching Hints

It should be noted that the footwork is identical for the Arch, Roll and Spin; the differences lie in the hand-to-hand contact, leads, and dance positions. The left-hand lead for the Spin In entails pulling the partner forward and turning her counterclockwise as the left-to-right-hand contact is released. The right-palm lead for the Spin Out is preceded by a release of the left-to-right-hand contact.

ARCH AND EXCHANGE

Position—One Hand (L to R)

Man's Part

Foot	Rhythm	Direction	Lead
1. L	S	Fwd (RTn)	LH High
2. R	S	Bwd	
3. L	q	Bwd	
4. R	q	IP	

Woman's Part

Foot	Rhythm	Direction
1. R	S	Fwd (LTn)
2. L	S	Bwd
3. R	q	Bwd
4. L	q	IP

Arch and Exchange

Teaching Hints

The woman's part of this step is the same as in the Arch In, while the man's part entails an exchange of positions with his partner. He does this by stepping forward past her right shoulder without turning his back to her. The lead consists of raising the left hand and pulling her forward under the arch. (See photographs.)

WALK BY

Position—One Hand (R to R)

Man's Part

Foot	Rhythm	Direction	Lead
1. L	S	Fwd (LTn)	RH Pull
2. R	S	Bwd	
3. L	q	Bwd	
4. R	q	IP	

Woman's Part

Foot	Rhythm	Direction
1. R	S	Fwd
2. L	S	Fwd (RTn)
3. R	q	Bwd
4. L	q	IP

Arch and Exchange

Teaching Hints

This step requires the dancers to exchange positions by passing right shoulders. This is done by the man turning his back to his partner while she simply steps forward and turns in. When this step is performed from a One-Hand Position with right-to-right-hand contact, the man generally switches to a left-to-right contact behind his back as he and his partner pass right shoulders.

The man can also lead into the Walk By from left-to-right contact by placing the woman's right hand on his shoulder. Then, as he turns, her hand runs across his shoulder and down his arm to his left hand. A third way to dance this step is by placing her hand at his waist and then completing the step. (See photographs.)

Shoulder Walk By

Waist Walk By

Walk By Behind Back

WRAP AND UNWRAP

Wrap

Position—Two Hand to Wrap

Man's Part

	Foot	Rhythm	Direction	Lead
1.	L	S	Fwd	LH Pull
2.	R	S	IP	
3.	L	q	Bwd	
4.	R	q	IP	

Woman's Part

	Foot	Rhythm	Direction
1.	R	S	Fwd (LTn)
2.	L	S	Bwd
3.	R	q	Bwd
4.	L	q	IP

Unwrap
Position—Wrap to Two Hand

Man's Part

	Foot	Rhythm	Direction	Lead
1.	L	S	Fwd	LH High
2.	R	S	IP	
3.	L	q	Bwd	
4.	R	q	IP	

Woman's Part

	Foot	Rhythm	Direction
1.	R	S	Fwd (RTn)
2.	L	S	Bwd
3.	R	q	Bwd
4.	L	q	IP

Teaching Hints

Essentially, the Unwrap consists of a basic step by the man and an Arch In and Arch Out by the woman. The man should raise his left hand to lead his partner to a side-by-side position. To unwrap, the man raises his left hand and leads the woman under the arch, or he may release her right hand and push her forward with his right forearm ending in a right-to-left One-Hand Position. (See photograph of Wrap Position in chapter 2.)

DOUBLE UNDER

Position—One Hand (L to R)

Man's Part

	Foot	Rhythm	Direction	Lead
1.	L	S	Fwd (LTn)	LH High
2.	R	S	Bwd	
3.	L	q	Bwd	
4.	R	q	IP	

Woman's Part

	Foot	Rhythm	Direction
1.	R	S	Fwd (LTn)
2.	L	S	Bwd
3.	R	q	Bwd
4.	L	q	IP

Double Under

Teaching Hints

This step consists of an Arch In by the woman and an Arch Step by the man to exchange positions. The man's raised left hand leads the woman forward under the arch on the first beat of the first slow step; on the second beat of the first step, the man passes under the arch. (See photograph.)

REVERSE SPIN

Position—One Hand (R to R)

Man's Part

	Foot	Rhythm	Direction	Lead
1.	L	S	Fwd	RH Push
2.	R	S	IP	
3.	L	q	Bwd	
4.	R	q	IP	

Woman's Part

	Foot	Rhythm	Direction
1.	R	S	Fwd X (R Spin)
2.	L	S	Sd
3.	R	q	Bwd
4.	L	q	IP

Teaching Hints

During this step the man performs the basic step while the woman spins. The Reverse Spin requires a strong, well-timed right-hand lead that consists of a pull on the first beat and a push (palm against palm) on the second beat of the first step. The woman must complete the spin (360°) on the first slow so that she can face her partner on the second slow and then rock on the quick steps. (See photographs.)

Reverse Spin

Reverse Spin

BEGINNINNG ROUTINES

The following routines are designed for dancing in one spot on the dance floor.

ROUTINE ONE

1. Rock Basic
2. Rock Basic
3. Arch (Out)
4. Arch (In)
5. Link
6. Link
7. Repeat

ROUTINE TWO

1. Link
2. Link
3. Roll (In)
4. Roll (Out)
5. Arch and Exchange
6. Butterfly
7. Butterfly
8. Repeat

ROUTINE THREE

1. Link
2. Walk By
3. Link
4. Double Under
5. Link
6. Roll (In)
7. Roll (Out)
8. Repeat

ROUTINE FOUR

1. Rock Basic
2. Arch (Out)
3. Arch (In)
4. Link
5. Spin
6. Link
7. Wrap and Unwrap
8. Link
9. Repeat

ADVANCED SECTION

This section includes eight steps written in SSqq rhythm. At this point, students should have mastered the Single Lindy so these steps can be performed in both the Single and Double Lindy style of Swing.

DOUBLE REVERSE SPIN

Position—One Hand (R to R)

Double Reverse Spin

Man's Part

	Foot	Rhythm	Direction	Lead
1.	L	S	Fwd (LSpin)	RH Push
2.	R	S	Sd	
3.	L	q	Bwd	
4.	R	q	IP	

Woman's Part

	Foot	Rhythm	Direction
1.	R	S	FwdX (RSpin)
2.	L	S	Sd
3.	R	q	Bwd
4.	L	q	IP

Teaching Hints

For this step the woman performs the Reverse Spin as described earlier, while the man spins counterclockwise and returns to a One-Hand Position. On the first beat of the first slow step, both dancers step forward, and on the second beat they spin 360° to face each other. The impetus for the spin comes from a right palm to a right-palm push on the second beat of the first slow step. (See photographs.)

DOUBLE ARCH

Position—Two Hand to Back to Back to Two Hand

Double Arch

Man's Part

	Foot	Rhythm	Direction	Lead
1.	L	S	Fwd X	LH Low & RH High
2.	R	S	Pv (RTn)	
3.	L	q	Sd	
4.	R	q	IP	

Woman's Part

	Foot	Rhythm	Direction
1.	R	S	Fwd X
2.	L	S	Pv (LTn)
3.	R	q	Sd
4.	L	q	IP

Double Arch

Teaching Hints

Also known as the Dishrag, this step entails stepping toward each other, turning back-to-back, and returning to a facing position. The man leads into this step by lowering his left hand and raising his right. (See photographs.)

WRAP WALK

Position—Wrap

Man's Part

	Foot	Rhythm	Direction	Lead
1.	L	S	Fwd	Body
2.	R	S	Fwd	
3.	L	q	Fwd	
4.	R	q	Fwd	

Woman's Part

	Foot	Rhythm	Direction
1.	R	S	Bwd
2.	L	S	Bwd
3.	R	q	Bwd
4.	L	q	Bwd

Teaching Hints

This step is done in the Wrap Position with the man walking forward and the woman backward in a clockwise direction. Once the students master this step they should learn this combination: Wrap (SSqq), Wrap Walk (qqqq), and Unwrap (SSqq). The six consecutive quick steps make this an attractive combination.

TWISTER

Position—Two Hand

Man's Part

	Foot	Rhythm	Direction	Lead
1.	L	S	Fwd (RPv)	Pull
2.	R	S	Bwd	
3.	L	q	Bwd	Push
4.	R	q	IP	

Woman's Part

	Foot	Rhythm	Direction
1.	R	S	FwdX (RPv)
2.	L	S	Fwd
3.	R	q	Bwd
4.	L	q	IP

Twister

Teaching Hints

This step is an advanced version of the Butterfly. On the first slow step, the dancers step forward to a right-shoulder-to-right-shoulder position and pivot 180° to a left-shoulder-to-left-shoulder position on the second step. The lead is a two-handed pull-and-push action by both dancers. (See photographs.)

GRAPEVINE

Position—Two Hand

Man's Part

	Foot	Rhythm	Direction	Lead
1.	L	S	FwdX	LH Pull
2.	R	S	Sd	
3.	L	q	BwdX	RH Pull
4.	R	q	Sd	

Woman's Part

	Foot	Rhythm	Direction
1.	R	S	FwdX
2.	L	S	Sd
3.	R	q	BwdX
4.	L	q	Sd

Twister

61

Teaching Hints

This attractive step moves the dancers laterally. The Grapevine can be done also to the man's left by dancing Sd, Fwd X, Sd, Bwd X. The dancers should follow a rule of crossing forward on the slow steps and backward on the quick steps. The hand lead is a waist-high pull in the direction of movement.

SWEETHEART

Position—One Hand (R to R) to Sweetheart

Man's Part

	Foot	Rhythm	Direction	Lead
1.	L	S	Fwd	RH Pull
2.	R	S	IP	
3.	L	q	Bwd	
4.	R	q	IP	

Woman's Part

	Foot	Rhythm	Direction
1.	R	S	Fwd (LTn 180°)
2.	L	S	Bwd
3.	R	q	Bwd
4.	L	q	IP

Teaching Hints

Basically, the Sweetheart entails an Arch In by the woman and a basic step by the man. The man leads the woman into the Sweetheart Position by raising his right hand and pulling her to his right side. As the woman turns, she raises her left hand and places it in his left hand. The couple may stay in the Sweetheart Position and do several basic steps before he releases her left hand and returns her to a right-to-right One-Hand Position.

KICK

Position—One Hand (L to L) to One Hand (R to R)

Man's Part

	Foot	Rhythm	Direction	Lead
1.	L	S	Fwd X (RTn 90°)	LH Pull
2.	R	S	K	
3.	L	q	Bwd	LH Push
4.	R	q	IP	
5.	L	S	Fwd (LTn 90°)	RH Pull
6.	R	S	K	
7.	L	q	Bwd	RH Push
8.	R	q	IP	

Woman's Part

	Foot	Rhythm	Direction
1.	R	S	Fwd (RTn 90°)
2.	L	S	K
3.	R	q	Bwd
4.	L	q	IP
5.	R	S	FwdX (LTn 90°)
6.	L	S	K
7.	R	q	Bwd
8.	L	q	IP

Teaching Hints

The kick portion of this step is performed in a side-by-side position with dancers facing opposite directions. The kick is done on the second slow step with one beat used for the actual kick and the second beat used for returning the foot to the floor. The man leads the woman into a side-by-side position with a pull and returns her to a facing position with a push. It may be advisable to add a Link Step between each kick. (See photographs.)

TOUCH WALK

Position—Open

Kick

Man's Part

	Foot	Rhythm	Direction	Lead
1.	L	S	Fwd	RH Pull
2.	R	S	Fwd	
3.	L	q	Fwd	
4.	R	q	Fwd	

Woman's Part

	Foot	Rhythm	Direction
1.	R	S	Fwd
2.	L	S	Fwd
3.	R	q	Fwd
4.	L	q	Fwd

Kick

Teaching Hints

This step is simply a walk in Double Lindy rhythm with the slow steps danced touch-step, touch-step. The touch and step take one beat each.

ADVANCED ROUTINES

These routines are spot routines that require a relatively small area for each couple on the dance floor.

ROUTINE ONE
1. Link
2. Double Reverse Spin
3. Link
4. Twister
5. Twister
6. Arch (Out)
7. Link
8. Repeat

ROUTINE TWO
1. Link
2. Double Arch
3. Link
4. Wrap
5. Wrap Walk
6. Unwrap
7. Link
8. Sweetheart (In)
9. Sweetheart (Out)
10. Repeat

ROUTINE THREE
1. Link
2. Grapevine (R)
3. Grapevine (L)
4. Link
5. Double Reverse Spin
6. Link
7. Wrap
8. Wrap Walk
9. Unwrap
10. Repeat

ROUTINE FOUR
1. Rock Basic
2. Touch Walk
3. Touch Walk
4. Arch Out (R to L)
5. Link
6. Kick (R)
7. Link
8. Kick (L)
9. Link
10. Repeat

6

the waltz

During the 18th century Austria became the hub around which all European music revolved. At that time the Austrian peasant dances called *Ländlers* were brought to the ballrooms, and there they developed into *Waltzers*, meaning sliding or gliding. As the Waltzer became more and more popular throughout Europe, its name was shortened to Waltz. Although the Waltz received much criticism because of its use of the Closed Dance Position, it survived to bring a whole new style to ballroom dancing.

As the popularity of the Waltz spread to Vienna, Johann Strauss began composing Waltz music with faster 3/4 tempos that increased the turning, spinning quality of the Waltz. The "Viennese Waltz" required a pivot spin on the third step which took much skill and endurance to execute.

Americans modified the "Viennese Waltz" by slowing down the 3/4 tempo and making all three beats even. This brought about a renewed interest in the Waltz, since the slower tempo with three even steps per measure encouraged dancers of all skill levels to attempt and experiment with the ever beautiful Waltz.

TEMPO

A moderate tempo is the most conducive to proper learning of the Waltz style. Beginners tend to rush the close step if the tempo is too slow. Between 90 and 120 beats per minute are comfortable for the beginner while

65

advanced dancers may prefer from 150 to 180 beats per minute.

RHYTHM

Written in 3/4 time, the Waltz requires three steps of equal duration per measure, which means that the lead foot changes on the first beat of each measure. This is why Waltz combinations and patterns are usually written in sets of six steps.

The music notation for the Waltz is written as follows:

3/4	♩ ♩ ♩	♩ ♩ ♩ ‖
Count	1 2 3	1 2 3
Rhythm	S S S	S S S

STEPS

The following steps are presented for the Waltz:

Beginner's Section: Waltz Basic, Travel, Left Turn, Right Turn, Hesitation, Crossover, Arch, and Wheel

Advanced Section: Left Pirouette Turn, Right Pirouette Turn, Backward Wheel, Unwrap, Cuddle Wheel, Scissors, and Weave

STYLING

The relaxed, gliding appearance of the Waltz is created by the erect posture of the dancers, coupled with long reaching steps that originate from their hips. These reaching steps are kept close to the floor for maximum smoothness and grace.

The rise and fall of the body is unique to the Waltz and essential for proper stylization. The first beat of the measure is accentuated with the fall which happens when the dancer steps flat on the foot and slightly bends or relaxes the knee. The rise follows as the dancer gently straightens the knee to step onto the ball of the foot for the next two beats.

Waltz partners should be reminded to continually strive for the feeling of oneness while dancing. For more in-depth styling techniques refer to chapter 2.

TEACHING THE WALTZ

Before attempting any steps or step patterns, the students must be able to readily distinguish the even 3/4 Waltz tempo. Begin by having the students individually walk the rhythm around the dance floor while verbally counting or clapping the beats. Then, demonstrate the Waltz Basic and direct students to practice it individually, facing the same direction. Remind the students that the lead foot changes on the first count of each measure and is always slightly accentuated.

Next, progress to the Open Position with partners holding inside hands, and have students practice the Waltz Basic until they feel comfortable with the step pattern and beat. Dancers then should move to the Closed Position at which time proper leading and following techniques should be stressed (refer to chapter 2). The man's body lead on steps one and four must be definite since it provides the directional indication for the woman.

Effective cuing when teaching is extremely important to the dancers' initial success and may be accomplished by using any one of the following: Fwd-Sd-Cl, 1-2-3, S-S-S, L-R-Cl—R-L-Cl, or L-2-3—R-2-3 (the opposite foot leads are used for the woman). This puts a word cue on each beat in the 3/4 tempo and helps the dancers identify the distinctive beat quality of the Waltz.

Turning figures are difficult to teach, and therefore correctly used verbal cues are of great help to both dancer and teacher. Two verbal cues for turning figures in the Waltz are: Turn-2-3 or Turn-Side-Close. When executing a turn from the Closed Position, dancers should be reminded to stay directly in front of each other in order to maintain the positive feeling of oneness.

As dancers become more proficient at the Waltz, the cue of Flat-Up-Up may be used to further develop the rise and fall so important to the Waltz style (refer to chapter 2). For simplicity, the Waltz steps presented in this chapter are written in a 1-2-3 rhythm pattern.

BEGINNING SECTION

WALTZ BASIC

Position—Closed

Man's Part

	Foot	Rhythm	Direction	Lead
1.	L	1	Fwd	Body
2.	R	2	Sd	
3.	L	3	Cl	
4.	R	1	Bwd	RH Palm
5.	L	2	Sd	
6.	R	3	Cl	

Woman's Part

	Foot	Rhythm	Direction
1.	R	1	Bwd
2.	L	2	Sd
3.	R	3	Cl
4.	L	1	Fwd
5.	R	2	Sd
6.	L	3	Cl

This basic step requires two measures of music and is essential to know since it is the foundation of all Waltz steps. Again, the body lead in step 1 and the pressure of the right hand and fingertips in step 4 are important for a smooth, flowing Waltz. Steps 1 through 3 are considered the forward half of the basic step, while steps 4 through 6 are considered the backward half.

TRAVEL

Position—Closed

Man's Part

	Foot	Rhythm	Direction	Lead
1.	L	1	Fwd	Body
2.	R	2	Sd	
3.	L	3	Cl	
4.	R	1	Fwd	Body
5.	L	2	Sd	
6.	R	3	Cl	

Woman's Part

	Foot	Rhythm	Direction
1.	R	1	Bwd
2.	L	2	Sd
3.	R	3	Cl
4.	L	1	Bwd
5.	R	2	Sd
6.	L	3	Cl

Teaching Hints

This step is designed to move the dancers across the floor with the man leading either forward or backward. The sideward steps for both dancers are slightly diagonal. For the man, step 2 is diagonal to his right and step 5 is diagonal to his left. It is just the opposite for the woman.

LEFT TURN

Position—Closed

Man's Part

	Foot	Rhythm	Direction	Lead
1.	L	1	Fwd (LTn)	Body
2.	R	2	Sd	RH Fingertips
3.	L	3	Cl	
4.	R	1	Bwd (LTn)	Body
5.	L	2	Sd	RH Fingertips
6.	R	3	Cl	

Woman's Part

	Foot	Rhythm	Direction
1.	R	1	Bwd (LTn)
2.	L	2	Sd
3.	R	3	Cl
4.	L	1	Fwd (LTn)
5.	R	2	Sd
6.	L	3	Cl

Teaching Hints

Turning left moves the dancers in a counterclockwise direction, and they should remember that the body lead is extremely important to establish the intended direction of the turn. On the man's forward step, his left toe is turned out while the woman's right toe is turned in so that their bodies can complete the quarter turn. Therefore, on the man's backward step, his right toe is turned in while the woman's left toe is turned out. The dancers should always look in the direction of the turn.

Before dancing as partners in the Closed Position, the students can practice the turn individually by moving in a straight line down the length of the floor. Cue the turn with "Turn-Side-Close" or "Flat-Up-Up" to reinforce the proper rise and fall required for the Waltz style.

RIGHT TURN

Position—Closed

Man's Part

	Foot	Rhythm	Direction	Lead
1.	L	1	Bwd (RTn)	RH Heel
2.	R	2	Sd	
3.	L	3	Cl	
4.	R	1	Fwd (RTn)	Body
5.	L	2	Sd	
6.	R	3	Cl	

Woman's Part

	Foot	Rhythm	Direction
1.	R	1	Fwd (RTn)
2.	L	2	Sd
3.	R	3	Cl
4.	L	1	Bwd (RTn)
5.	R	2	Sd
6.	L	3	Cl

Teaching Hints

The Right Turn moves the dancers clockwise and is executed in the same manner as the Left Turn. Dancers must remember that the feet lead the body in the direction of the turn and to always look right while turning. This turn is difficult for beginners because of its clockwise direction. Therefore, the dancers may find it easier to lead into a Right Turn by executing the forward half of the Waltz Basic and then to begin with step 4 as given above.

HESITATION

Position—Closed

Man's Part

	Foot	Rhythm	Direction	Lead
1.	L	1	Fwd	Body
2.	R	2	Tc	RH Lift
3.	L	3	Ho	
4.	R	1	Bwd	RH Palm
5.	L	2	Tc	RH Lift
6.	R	3	Ho	

Woman's Part

	Foot	Rhythm	Direction
1.	R	1	Bwd
2.	L	2	Tc
3.	R	3	Ho
4.	L	1	Fwd
5.	R	2	Tc
6.	L	3	Ho

Teaching Hints

The Hesitation can be performed beginning forward, backward, or from side-to-side. Its steps tend to be slightly smaller than those of the Waltz Basic but its rhythm is constant. The Hesitation can be used as a link between two different figures. For example, partners could begin turning left for a number of measures and then insert the Hesitation Step before beginning to turn right. Dancers must remember that there is no transfer of weight on the touch steps, but there is a definite lift in the body as the toe is brought to the heel.

CROSSOVER

Position—Closed to Semi-Open to Closed

Man's Part

	Foot	Rhythm	Direction	Lead
1.	L	1	Fwd	Body
2.	R	2	Sd	
3.	L	3	Cl	
4.	R	1	FwdX	RH Heel
5.	L	2	Sd	Fingertips
6.	R	3	Cl	

Woman's Part

	Foot	Rhythm	Direction
1.	R	1	Bwd
2.	L	2	Sd
3.	R	3	Cl
4.	L	1	Fwd X
5.	R	2	Sd
6.	L	3	Cl

Teaching Hints

In step 4 the dancers assume a Semi-Open Position with hips adjacent, while in steps 5 and 6 they turn toward each other ending in the Closed Position. Dancers may stay in the Semi-Open Position after step 4, returning to the Closed Position with the woman's execution of a 180° turn on step 1.

ARCH

Position—Arch

Man's Part

	Foot	Rhythm	Direction	Lead
1.	L	1	Fwd	LH High & RH Palm
2.	R	2	Sd	
3.	L	3	Cl	
4.	R	1	Fwd	Body
5.	L	2	Sd	
6.	R	3	Cl	

Woman's Part

	Foot	Rhythm	Direction
1.	R	1	Fwd (RTn)
2.	L	2	Sd
3.	R	3	Cl
4.	L	1	Bwd
5.	R	2	Sd
6.	L	3	Cl

Teaching Hints

When raising the woman's right arm, the man should lead strongly with his right hand to assure her of the intended direction. He must also continue his forward movement in order to keep the flowing continuity between him and his partner.

WHEEL

Position—Right Side

Man's Part

	Foot	Rhythm	Direction	Lead
1.	L	1	Fwd	Body
2.	R	2	Fwd	
3.	L	3	Fwd	
4.	R	1	Fwd	
5.	L	2	Fwd	
6.	R	3	Fwd	

Woman's Part

	Foot	Rhythm	Direction
1.	R	1	Fwd
2.	L	2	Fwd
3.	R	3	Fwd
4.	L	1	Fwd
5.	R	2	Fwd
6.	L	3	Fwd

Teaching Hints

To move into any Side Position, the man's lead must be firm with both dancers responding immediately by stepping forward into position. Dancers should look at each other while turning.

BEGINNING ROUTINES

ROUTINE ONE

1. Waltz Basic
2. Waltz Basic
3. Crossover
4. Hesitation
5. Left Turn
6. Left Turn
7. Repeat in reverse direction

ROUTINE TWO

1. Waltz Basic
2. Waltz Basic
3. Right Turn
4. Right Turn
5. Waltz Basic
6. Arch
7. Repeat in reverse direction

ROUTINE THREE

1. Waltz Basic
2. Arch
3. Wheel (180°)
4. Wheel (180°)
5. Waltz Basic
6. Hesitation
7. Repeat in reverse direction

ROUTINE FOUR

1. Left Turn
2. Crossover
3. Hesitation
4. Right Turn
5. Crossover
6. Waltz Basic
7. Repeat

ADVANCED SECTION

LEFT PIROUETTE TURN

Position—Closed to Right Side

Man's Part

	Foot	Rhythm	Direction	Lead
1.	L	1	Fwd (LTn)	Body
2.	R	2	Tc	
3.	L	3	Ho	
4.	R	1	Bwd	
5.	L	2	Bwd	
6.	R	3	Cl	

Woman's Part

	Foot	Rhythm	Direction
1.	R	1	Bwd (LTn)
2.	L	2	Tc
3.	R	3	Ho
4.	L	1	Fwd
5.	R	2	Fwd
6.	L	3	Cl

Teaching Hints

This Pirouette Turn is danced with a left turn of 180°. To help maintain balance on this pivoting turn, dancers should remember to keep their bodies erect and in direct line with each other. Steps 4, 5, and 6 may be danced forward for the man and backward for the woman.

RIGHT PIROUETTE TURN

Position—Closed to Left Side

Man's Part

	Foot	Rhythm	Direction	Lead
1.	L	1	Fwd (RTn)	Body
2.	R	2	Tc	
3.	L	3	Ho	
4.	R	1	Bwd	
5.	L	2	Bwd	
6.	R	3	Cl	

Woman's Part

	Foot	Rhythm	Direction
1.	R	1	Bwd (RTn)
2.	L	2	Tc
3.	R	3	Ho
4.	L	1	Fwd
5.	R	2	Fwd
6.	L	3	Cl

Teaching Hints

This right turn, which should be one of 180°, is easily executed after a forward half of the Waltz Basic. For added style, dancers should look at each other when turning. Steps 4, 5, and 6 may be danced forward for the man and backward for the woman.

BACKWARD WHEEL

Position—Closed to Sweetheart

Man's Part

	Foot	Rhythm	Direction	Lead
1.	L	1	Bwd	LH High
2.	R	2	Sd	RH to RH
3.	L	3	Cl	
4.	R	1	Bwd	
5.	L	2	Fwd (RTn)	
6.	R	3	Fwd (RTn)	

Teaching Hints   **Woman's Part**

	Foot	Rhythm	Direction
1.	R	1	Fwd
2.	L	2	Bwd
3.	R	3	Cl
4.	L	1	Bwd
5.	R	2	Bwd
6.	L	3	Bwd

Teaching Hints

This step begins by dancing the forward half of the Waltz Basic. As the backward half begins, the man immediately leads the woman into his right side with an exchange of hands (R to R) to end in a Sweetheart Position with both partners facing the same direction. The man acts as the pivot point, keeping his steps small while his right hand leads strongly to indicate the woman's backward movement. To move out of this position, the Unwrap Step may be used.

UNWRAP

Position—Sweetheart to Closed

Man's Part

	Foot	Rhythm	Direction	Lead
1.	L	1	Fwd	LH High
2.	R	2	Fwd	
3.	L	3	Cl	
4.	R	1	Fwd	Body
5.	L	2	Sd	
6.	R	3	Cl	

Woman's Part

	Foot	Rhythm	Direction
1.	R	1	Fwd (RTn)
2.	L	2	Bwd
3.	R	3	Cl
4.	L	1	Bwd
5.	R	2	Sd
6.	L	3	Cl

Teaching Hints

The woman is on the man's right side in Sweetheart Position as he leads into the Unwrap by raising his left arm. In step 3 the dancers change to a one-hand position, man's left to woman's right. The slight pull of the man's left hand brings both partners back to Closed Position. The woman should always look in the direction of her 180° turn.

CUDDLE WHEEL

Position—Closed to Wrap

Man's Part

	Foot	Rhythm	Direction	Lead
1.	L	1	Bwd	LH High
2.	R	2	Bwd	
3.	L	3	Cl	
4.	R	1	Bwd (LTn)	Body
5.	L	2	Bwd (LTn)	
6.	R	3	Cl	

Woman's Part

	Foot	Rhythm	Direction
1.	R	1	Fwd (LTn)
2.	L	2	Bwd
3.	R	3	Cl
4.	L	1	Fwd (LTn)
5.	R	2	Fwd (LTn)
6.	L	3	Cl

Teaching Hints

The Cuddle Wheel begins as the man leads the woman to his right side by crossing his high left hand in front of him and turning her under his arm. At the same time, the woman's left hand drops to waist level to grasp the man's right hand. Now in Wrap Position, both facing the same direction, the man acts as a pivot point by leading the woman forward as he moves backward while turning left to execute the Wheel. To move out of this position, the Unwrap may be used but also encourage dancers to experiment with different ways.

Scissors

Scissors

SCISSORS

Position—Right Side to Left Side

Man's Part

	Foot	Rhythm	Direction	Lead
1.	L	1	Fwd	Body
2.	R	2	Fwd	
3.	L	3	Cl (PvR)	RH Heel
4.	R	1	Fwd	Body
5.	L	2	Fwd	
6.	R	3	Cl (PvL)	RH Fingertips

Woman's Part

	Foot	Rhythm	Direction
1.	R	1	Bwd
2.	L	2	Bwd
3.	R	3	Cl (PvR)
4.	L	1	Bwd
5.	R	2	Bwd
6.	L	3	Cl(PvL)

Teaching Hints

This step is done in a zigzag fashion, and when repeated several times, it looks very elegant. Dancers should remember to complete this step on an even number of repetitions so that a new step can be started with the left foot for the man and the right for the woman. Also, the partners must turn slightly toward each other on steps 2 and 3 of the last repetition so that they are ready for the new step. This can begin from a Left Side Position as well. (See photographs.)

WEAVE

Position—Reverse to Semi-Open

Man's Part

	Foot	Rhythm	Direction	Lead
1.	L	1	Fwd X	LH High
2.	R	2	Sd	
3.	L	3	Cl	
4.	R	1	Fwd X	RH Heel
5.	L	2	Sd	
6.	R	3	Cl	

Woman's Part

	Foot	Rhythm	Direction
1.	R	1	Fwd X
2.	L	2	Sd
3.	R	3	Cl
4.	L	1	Fwd X
5.	R	2	Sd
6.	L	3	Cl

Teaching Hints

On the forward cross step the man's left hand crosses in front of his body and leads the woman to the Semi-Open Position. On the next cross step, the man may lead either by placing his right hand around the woman's waist or by grasping her left hand for the pull across as on the initial forward cross. The Weave may also begin after the forward half of the Waltz Basic.

ADVANCED ROUTINES

ROUTINE ONE

1. Waltz Basic (Fwd Half)
2. Left Pirouette Turn
3. Right Pirouette Turn
4. Waltz Basic
5. Backward Wheel
6. Unwrap
7. Repeat in reverse
   direction

ROUTINE TWO

1. Waltz Basic
2. Weave
3. Weave
4. Waltz Basic
5. Cuddle Wheel
6. Unwrap
7. Repeat in reverse
   direction

ROUTINE THREE

1. Scissors
2. Waltz Basic
3. Backward Wheel
4. Unwrap
5. Travel
6. Left Pirouette Turn
7. Right Pirouette Turn
8. Repeat in reverse
   direction

ROUTINE FOUR

1. Scissors
2. Cuddle Wheel
3. Unwrap
4. Travel
5. Weave
6. Weave
7. Repeat in reverse
   direction

the cha-cha

A Latin American influence in music and dance became evident during the 1940s when Havana, Cuba, was a popular resort spot for Americans. Musicians who played in the nightclubs developed the Mambo rhythm out of a combination of American Jazz and the Cuban Rumba. A dance was created to fit this Mambo, but because it had an offbeat rhythm, it was danced mostly by those familiar with intricate Afro-Cuban music.

The Cha-Cha evolved from a Mambo figure which consisted of two slow steps followed by three quick changes of weight. These three quick steps gave the dance its frequently used name, Cha-Cha-Cha. This syncopated rhythm replaced the offbeat rhythm of the Mambo, making it easier for the ballroom dancer to adjust to the Latin American tempo and style of dancing.

TEMPO

A moderate tempo between 128 to 140 beats per minute is comfortable for dancing the Cha-Cha. The unique style of the Cha-Cha tends to lose its quality with any faster tempo.

RHYTHM

Music for the Cha-Cha is written in 4/4 time with the third beat split into two eighth notes. The music notation for the Cha-Cha is written as follows:

4/4										
Count	1-2	3-4	5, 6	7-8		1-2	3-4	5, 6	7-8	
Rhythm	S	S	q q	S		S	S	q q	S	

STEPS

The steps included for the Cha-Cha are:

Beginner's Section: Cha-Cha Basic, Crossover, Half Chase, Side Rock, Alternate Cross, Full Chase, Kick

Advanced Section: Traveling Touch, Back Break, Roll In-Roll Out, Double Crossover, Full Turn, Crossover Turn

STYLING

Much of the Cha-Cha's styling is similar to that of the Rumba and Mambo. Cuban dances are smooth and the feet do all the work with minimum upper body movement. Each step is small and close to the floor while the knees and pelvis are kept relaxed. Dancers should keep their weight on the insides of their feet with their knees forward.

Because the majority of the movement is created from the waist down, the arms and hands are free to express the natural body rhythm felt by each dancer. However, the arms are always kept slightly flexed to maintain the stylish appearance of the Cha-Cha.

This dance remains somewhat stationary and is danced most frequently in a Free Position, allowing dancers maximum freedom of movement and creativity. The Cha-Cha is danced also in Closed and Link Positions and moves with a diagonal, in-place, or traveling floor pattern.

TEACHING THE CHA-CHA

With all dancers facing the same direction and using the same footwork, begin marking time in place. Check that everyone is making five changes of weight per measure so that the next figure can begin with the opposite footwork. Dancers may be clapping or verbally counting the rhythm as it is practiced. After the dancers are thoroughly familiar with the rhythm, add music until the footwork and rhythm are coordinated. Be certain to choose music with a distinct rhythm. As new positions and steps are taught, always begin by having the students practice them individually, all facing in the same direction.

Remind dancers that there should be a feeling of resistance as they shift their body weight forward and backward. Also, they should be reminded to keep their weight on the insides of their feet. Have students practice in-place and traveling floor patterns. Encourage students to experiment with other positions, thus giving the Cha-Cha their personal flare.

When beginning dancers are in Free Position, the man often has difficulty leading because of the lack of physical contact. Consequently, subtle hand and body leads should be developed for each dance step. For example, a slight flick of the right hand is a good lead for the Crossover to the man's right while a flick of the left hand is the lead for a Crossover to his left. To assist the beginner, allow verbal communication when necessary but always encourage the practice of visual cues. Beginners may find it helpful to dance with the same partner for a number of lessons.

Verbal cues assist the teacher in keeping the class together when new steps are being taught. With the students practicing as a unit, the teacher can scan the room to easily detect any initial problems that can be corrected immediately. This also helps keep the class at a somewhat common learning pace although the teacher must adjust to varied abilities. Furthermore, cues that correctly coincide with the music enable students to feel the rhythm and step patterns better. In addition to the cues suggested for each step, the following two may also be used: 1-2-Cha-Cha-Cha or Slow-Slow-Cha-Cha-Slow.

The progression of dance steps for advanced dancers can be somewhat faster. The following preparatory figure is often used with advanced students: Sd(S), Bwd(S), Fwd(S), Fwd(q), Fwd(q), Fwd(S). Just as the Basic Step is used between dance steps for the beginner, this figure acts as a link between dance steps for the advanced student.

BEGINNING SECTION

CHA-CHA BASIC

Position—Free

Man's Part

	Foot	Rhythm	Direction	Lead
1.	L	S	Fwd	Body
2.	R	S	IP	
3.	L	q	Bwd	
4.	R	q	Bwd	
5.	L	S	Bwd	
6.	R	S	Bwd	Body
7.	L	S	IP	
8.	R	q	Fwd	
9.	L	q	Fwd	
10.	R	S	Fwd	

Woman's Part

	Foot	Rhythm	Direction
1.	R	S	Bwd
2.	L	S	IP
3.	R	q	Fwd
4.	L	q	Fwd
5.	R	S	Fwd
6.	L	S	Fwd
7.	R	S	IP
8.	L	q	Bwd
9.	R	q	Bwd
10.	L	S	Bwd

Teaching Hints

The first two slow steps of the Basic consist of a rocking movement forward and backward. Students should practice this rocking move individually before completing the entire Basic Step. Step 6 begins a second Cha-Cha figure moving in the opposite direction.

CROSSOVER

Position—One Hand

Man's Part

	Foot	Rhythm	Direction	Lead
1.	L	S	Fwd X	LH Pull
2.	R	S	IP	
3.	L	q	Sd	
4.	R	q	Cl	
5.	L	S	Sd	

Woman's Part

	Foot	Rhythm	Direction
1.	R	S	Fwd X
2.	L	S	IP
3.	R	q	Sd
4.	L	q	Cl
5.	R	S	Sd

Teaching Hints

The man's left-hand lead must be strong to indicate the proper direction of the first slow crossover movement. Dancers should face the direction in which they crossed, and on the quick steps, return to a facing position until the end of the figure. As this step repeats, the dancers must change to the opposite one-hand position to repeat the Crossover to the man's left. (See photographs.)

Crossover

Crossover

HALF CHASE

Position—Free

Man's Part

	Foot	Rhythm	Direction	Lead
1.	L	S	Fwd	Body
2.	R	S	IP(LTn)	
3.	L	q	Fwd	
4.	R	q	Fwd	
5.	L	S	Fwd	
6.	R	S	Fwd	Body
7.	L	S	IP (RTn)	
8.	R	q	Fwd	
9.	L	q	Fwd	
10.	R	S	Fwd	

Half Chase

Woman's Part

	Foot	Rhythm	Direction
1.	R	S	Bwd
2.	L	S	IP
3.	R	q	Fwd
4.	L	q	Fwd
5.	R	S	Fwd
6.	L	S	Fwd
7.	R	S	IP
8.	L	q	Bwd
9.	R	q	Bwd
10.	L	S	Bwd

Half Chase

Teaching Hints

Turns are usually made on the slow steps and are executed either in place or traveling. If the turns are made on the quick steps, they should be done in place. The shoulders and upper body initiate each turn while the force applied by the dancer determines the degree. In the above figure, the half turns may be executed by either the man or woman. The Chase occurs after this turn when both dancers are facing the same direction. (See photographs.)

Half Chase

SIDE ROCK

Position—One-Hand (Left to Right)

Man's Part

	Foot	Rhythm	Direction	Lead
1.	L	S	Sd	LH Pull L
2.	R	S	IP	
3.	L	q	Cl	
4.	R	q	IP	
5.	L	S	IP	

Half Chase

Woman's Part

	Foot	Rhythm	Direction
1.	R	S	Sd
2.	L	S	IP
3.	R	q	Cl
4.	L	q	IP
5.	R	S	IP

Teaching Hints

The sideward steps are rocking steps, and the dancers should remember to keep their knees slightly relaxed and their feet close to the ground. This will help maintain the proper style of the Cha-Cha. The man may initiate a Side Rock to his right by pulling (LH) to his right.

ALTERNATE CROSS

Position—Closed to Left Side to Closed

Man's Part

	Foot	Rhythm	Direction	Lead
1.	L	S	Fwd X	Body, RH Heel
2.	R	S	IP	
3.	L	q	Sd	RH Fingertips
4.	R	q	Cl	
5.	L	S	Sd	
6.	R	S	Bwd X	RH Palm
7.	L	S	IP	
8.	R	q	Sd	RH Fingertips
9.	L	q	Cl	
10.	R	S	Sd	

Woman's Part

	Foot	Rhythm	Direction
1.	R	S	Bwd X
2.	L	S	IP
3.	R	q	Sd
4.	L	q	Cl
5.	R	S	Sd
6.	L	S	Fwd X
7.	R	S	IP
8.	L	q	Sd
9.	R	q	Cl
10.	L	S	Sd

Teaching Hints

Partners turn slightly to their rights on the first slow step to step into a Left Side Position before returning to a Closed Position on the second slow step. Steps 6 through 10 are executed in the same manner except that, in step 6, the dancers turn slightly to their right, bringing them to a Left Side Position before they return to a Closed Position in step 7 to finish the figure.

FULL CHASE

Position—Free

Full Chase

Man's Part

	Foot	Rhythm	Direction	Lead
1.	L	S	Fwd	Body
2.	R	S	IP (LTn)	Body
3.	L	q	Fwd	
4.	R	q	Fwd	
5.	L	S	Fwd	
6.	R	S	Fwd	Body
7.	L	S	IP (RTn)	Body
8.	R	q	Fwd	
9.	L	q	Fwd	
10.	R	S	Fwd	

Full Chase

Woman's Part

	Foot	Rhythm	Direction
1.	R	S	Bwd
2.	L	S	IP
3.	R	q	Fwd
4.	L	q	Fwd
5.	R	S	Fwd
6.	L	S	Fwd
7.	R	S	IP (LTn)
8.	L	q	Fwd
9.	R	q	Fwd
10.	L	S	Fwd

Full Chase

Teaching Hints

All turns in this step are 180°, therefore, in step 7 both dancers are turning 180° simultaneously. The Full Chase ends with partners facing the same direction. To return to their original facing position, the woman must execute a 180° left turn in the next figure. Remember, the woman is visually cued by the man's body to execute the Full Chase. (See photographs.)

Full Chase

KICK

Position—Free

Man's Part

	Foot	Rhythm	Direction	Lead
1.	L	S	Fwd	Body
2.	R	S	K	
3.	R	q	Bwd	
4.	L	q	Bwd	
5.	R	S	Bwd	
6.	L	S	Bwd	Body
7.	R	S	K	
8.	R	q	Fwd	
9.	L	q	Fwd	
10.	R	S	Fwd	

Woman's Part

	Foot	Rhythm	Direction
1.	R	S	Bwd
2.	L	S	K
3.	L	q	Fwd
4.	R	q	Fwd
5.	L	S	Fwd
6.	R	S	Fwd
7.	L	S	K
8.	L	q	Bwd
9.	R	q	Bwd
10.	L	S	Bwd

Teaching Hints

In step 2 the man is kicking forward and the woman is kicking backward. The kick in step 7 is just the opposite, with the man kicking backward and the woman kicking forward.

BEGINNING ROUTINES

ROUTINE ONE

1. Cha-Cha Basic
2. Cha-Cha Basic
3. Crossover
4. Crossover
5. Half Chase
6. Half Chase
7. Kick
8. Repeat

ROUTINE TWO

1. Cha-Cha Basic
2. Cha-Cha Basic
3. Alternate Cross
4. Alternate Cross
5. Kick
6. Crossover
7. Crossover
8. Full Chase
9. Repeat

ROUTINE THREE

1. Cha-Cha Basic
2. Cha-Cha Basic
3. Kick
4. Half Chase
5. Half Chase
6. Side Rock
7. Side Rock
8. Repeat

ROUTINE FOUR

1. Cha-Cha Basic
2. Full Chase
3. Full Chase
4. Side Rock
5. Side Rock
6. Side Cross
7. Crossover
8. Repeat

ADVANCED SECTION

TRAVELING TOUCH

Position—One Hand (Left to Right)

Man's Part

	Foot	Rhythm	Direction	Lead
1.	L	S	Fwd	LH Push
2.	R	S	Fwd	
3.	L	q	Sd	LH Hold
4.	R	q	Cl	
5.	L	S	Tc	

Woman's Part

	Foot	Rhythm	Direction
1.	R	S	Bwd
2.	L	S	Bwd
3.	R	q	Sd
4.	L	q	Cl
5.	R	S	Tc

Teaching Hints

This step repeats with the same lead foot because there is no transfer of weight on the touch step. The figure may begin with the man moving backward on steps 1 and 2 while the woman moves forward; the figure can also be done in Free Position.

DOUBLE CROSSOVER

Position—One Hand (Left to Right)

Man's Part

	Foot	Rhythm	Direction	Lead
1.	L	S	Fwd X	LH Pull R
2.	R	S	Fwd X	LH Pull L
3.	L	q	Sd	
4.	R	q	Cl	
5.	L	S	Sd	

Woman's Part

	Foot	Rhythm	Direction
1.	R	S	Fwd X
2.	L	S	Fwd X
3.	R	q	Sd
4.	L	q	Cl
5.	R	S	Sd

Teaching Hints

On the forward cross steps, dancers turn slightly toward the direction of the cross. This step may be repeated beginning with the opposite feet.

BACK BREAK

Position—One Hand (Right to Left) to Full Open

Man's Part

	Foot	Rhythm	Direction	Lead
1.	L	S	Bwd	RH Push
2.	R	S	IP (LTn)	RH Pull
3.	L	q	Sd	
4.	R	q	Cl	
5.	L	S	IP	
6.	R	S	Bwd	
7.	L	S	IP (RTn)	
8.	R	q	Sd	
9.	L	q	Cl	
10.	R	S	IP	

Woman's Part

	Foot	Rhythm	Direction
1.	R	S	Bwd
2.	L	S	IP (RTn)
3.	R	q	Sd
4.	L	q	Cl
5.	R	S	IP
6.	L	S	Bwd
7.	R	S	IP (LTn)
8.	L	q	Sd
9.	R	q	Cl
10.	L	S	IP

Teaching Hints

This step ends with dancers in Full Open Position, woman on the man's right. Step 2 is a 90° turn and calls for a strong lead by the man. As this step repeats (steps 6-10), dancers must turn in the opposite direction on step 7 to return to their original facing position.

FULL TURN

Position—Free

Man's Part

	Foot	Rhythm	Direction	Lead
1.	L	S	Fwd	Body
2.	R	S	IP (LTn)	
3.	L	q	Bwd	
4.	R	q	IP	
5.	L	S	IP	

Woman's Part

	Foot	Rhythm	Direction
1.	R	S	Bwd
2.	L	S	IP (RTn)
3.	R	q	Fwd
4.	L	q	IP
5.	R	S	IP

Teaching Hints

To ensure a smooth, graceful Full Turn, the dancer should stay on the ball of the turning foot and always maintain an upright body position. Helpful cues for this step are "Ready-Turn-Cha-Cha-Cha" or "Slow-Turn-Cha-Cha-Cha." The 360° spin on step 2 may be executed in either direction.

ROLL IN - ROLL OUT

Position—One Hand (Right to Left)

Man's Part

	Foot	Rhythm	Direction	Lead
1.	L	S	Fwd	RH Pull
2.	R	S	IP	
3.	L	q	Bwd	
4.	R	q	Bwd	
5.	L	S	Bwd	
6.	R	S	Bwd	RH Pull
7.	L	S	IP	
8.	R	q	Fwd	
9.	L	q	Fwd	
10.	R	S	Fwd	

Woman's Part

	Foot	Rhythm	Direction
1.	R	S	Fwd
2.	L	S	IP (LTn)
3.	R	q	Bwd
4.	L	q	Bwd
5.	R	S	Bwd
6.	L	S	Bwd
7.	R	S	IP (RTn)
8.	L	q	Bwd
9.	R	q	Bwd
10.	L	S	Bwd

Roll In

Roll In

Teaching Hints

As the Roll In (steps 1-5) is executed, the held hands wrap around the woman's waist. After making a 180° turn on step 2, she ends on the man's right side, facing the same direction. As the Roll Out (steps 6-10) is executed, the woman turns 180° to her right on step 7, bringing the partners back to their original One-Hand Position. (See photographs.)

CROSSOVER TURN

Position—Free

Man's Part

	Foot	Rhythm	Direction	Lead
1.	L	S	FwdX (RTn)	Body
2.	R	S	IP (RTn)	
3.	L	q	Sd	
4.	R	q	Cl	
5.	L	S	S	
6.	R	S	FwdX (LTn)	Body
7.	L	S	IP (LTn)	
8.	R	q	Sd	
9.	L	q	Cl	
10.	R	S	Sd	

Woman's Part

	Foot	Rhythm	Direction
1.	R	S	FwdX (LTn)
2.	L	S	IP (LTn)
3.	R	q	Sd
4.	L	q	Cl
5.	R	S	Sd
6.	L	S	FwdX (RTn)
7.	R	S	IP (RTn)
8.	L	q	Sd
9.	R	q	Cl
10.	L	S	Sd

Teaching Hints

All turns in this step are 180° which means that on step 1 dancers will be back-to-back. Step 2 brings them face-to-face for the remainder of the figure. Dancers should remember to look over their shoulders at each other when executing step 1.

ADVANCED ROUTINES

ROUTINE ONE

1. Full Turn
2. Full Turn
3. Traveling Touch
4. Traveling Touch
5. Double Crossover
6. Double Crossover
7. Repeat

ROUTINE TWO

1. Traveling Touch
2. Traveling Touch
3. Roll In-Roll Out
4. Roll In-Roll Out
5. Back Break
6. Back Break
7. Crossover Turn
8. Crossover Turn
9. Repeat

ROUTINE THREE

1. Double Crossover
2. Double Crossover
3. Back Break
4. Back Break
5. Crossover Turn
6. Crossover Turn
7. Traveling Touch
8. Roll In-Roll Out
9. Repeat

ROUTINE FOUR

1. Roll In-Roll Out
2. Double Crossover
3. Back Break
4. Back Break
5. Crossover Turn
6. Crossover Turn
7. Traveling Touch
8. Repeat

8

the rumba

The stylish Rumba evolved from a combination of popular Cuban dances. These include the native Cuban Danzon of slow tempo, the Bolero and the Son of medium tempo, the Guaracha of fast tempo, and the rural Rumba originally danced as an imitation of movements done by barnyard animals. Since these Cuban dances sprang from African and Spanish influences, the beat of the music is often accented by rhythmic sounds of bongos or various drums, claves, maracas or timbales, while the melody usually carries a Spanish flavor.

The American style of Rumba extracted from these Cuban dances was introduced in the United States in 1930. It has remained a popular ballroom dance due to its interesting musical rhythm and fascinating style.

TEMPO

The American Rumba may be played and danced in slow, moderate, or fast tempo. To master any of the Latin American dances, the beginner should become familiar with the unique dominant beat of the music before proceeding with the step patterns. A comfortable tempo for the beginner is between 120 and 140 beats per minute. Faster tempos require the advanced dancer's skill in order to maintain the Rumba's exciting style.

RHYTHM

Musically, the American Rumba is written in either 2/4 or 4/4 time, and in both cases, the basic rhythm is arranged in counts of four. The basic Rumba step consists of three steps per measure with a "hold" or "wait" on the second beat. In 4/4 time this would take one measure while in 2/4 time it would take two measures to complete the same. Two measures in each time signature would be written as follows:

4/4	♩♩♩♩ | ♩♩♩♩ ‖
Count	1-2 3 4 1-2 3 4
Rhythm	S q q S q q

2/4	♩ ♩♩ | ♩ ♩♩ ‖
Count	1-2 3 4 1-2 3 4
Rhythm	S q q S q q

STEPS

The steps included for the Rumba are:

Beginner's Section: Rumba Basic, Left Turn, Arch Travel, Chassé, Back Cross, Front Cross, Reverse Wheel, Side Break

Advanced Section: Bolero Break, Wrap, Unwrap, Break Away, Open Walk Turn, Rock

STYLING

Characteristic of the Rumba is the subtle swaying of the dancer's hips while the upper body remains relatively quiet. Because this hip action is a direct result of the footwork, it is important that the dancer concentrate on the details of footwork first. Steps should be small and flat on the floor, enabling the knees to stay slightly relaxed while the pelvis shifts from side to side.

The Rumba pattern of Slow-quick-quick involves these essential factors: (1) dancers do not place any weight on count 1 of the slow step; (2) count 2 of the slow step assumes the weight as the same knee straightens; (3) as the knee straightens, the same hip will rise thus creating the desired hip action; and (4) since the quick steps take only one beat each, the action is faster but always flowing.

Throughout the Rumba, the upper body is relaxed but controlled, and the arms are free to express the natural movement felt by the individual dancer. Because of the Rumba's small steps, it is not a traveling dance but remains in a limited area with occasional traveling figures inserted for variety.

TEACHING THE RUMBA

A beginner's success with the Rumba starts with a clear understanding of the musical rhythm. Therefore, students should begin by walking this rhythm around the floor in a slow 4/4 time. This should be done on an individual basis, moving both forward and backward and keeping two beats to every step. Students should then progress to walking in partners, using a Full Open Position and eventually working into a Closed Position.

THE WALK

Position—Closed

Man's Part

	Foot	Rhythm	Direction	Lead
1.	L	S	Fwd	Body
2.	R	S	Fwd	
3.	L	S	Fwd	
4.	R	S	Fwd	

Woman's Part

	Foot	Rhythm	Direction
1.	R	S	Bwd
2.	L	S	Bwd
3.	R	S	Bwd
4.	L	S	Bwd

After the Walk is mastered, students should proceed to practice the Slow-quick-quick. When demonstrating these steps, the teacher should remember to face the same direction as the class in order to minimize confusion.

To develop the subtle swaying of the hips, the students should stand holding their hands on their hips and then begin shifting weight from the left to the right leg, remembering that the knee of the leg assuming the full weight must be relaxed and bent. As the weight transfer occurs, the students' hands on their hips will feel the shifting movement of the pelvis. Remind students that the transfer of weight should flow from one leg to the other to achieve the swaying quality. They should anticipate the transfer by starting to move the hips in the opposite direction just before the change is made.

After the weight transfer is learned, have the students practice adding it to the rhythm. They should keep the hip movement flowing through count 1 even though no transfer of weight is made there. The verbal cue of Step(1)-Hold(2)-Quick(3)-Quick(4) is helpful when practicing this.

Sufficient room should always be allowed between couples and individuals during practice. If full length mirrors are available, they will help correct faults not otherwise noticed. Also, if video-tape equipment is available, the teacher should film the students as they dance. Watching playbacks will help the students see how they can improve their movements and posture.

BEGINNING SECTION

RUMBA BASIC

Position—Closed

Man's Part

	Foot	Rhythm	Direction	Lead
1.	L	S	Fwd	Body
2.	R	q	Sd	
3.	L	q	Cl	
4.	R	S	Bwd	RH Palm
5.	L	q	Sd	
6.	R	q	Cl	

Woman's Part

	Foot	Rhythm	Direction
1.	R	S	Bwd
2.	L	q	Sd
3.	R	q	Cl
4.	L	S	Fwd
5.	R	q	Sd
6.	L	q	Cl

Teaching Hints

This step may begin with the quick steps, moving the dancers sideward on their first step (q-q-S pattern). They should keep all steps small and accentuate the hip movement.

LEFT TURN

Position—Closed

Man's Part

	Foot	Rhythm	Direction	Lead
1.	L	S	Fwd (LTn)	Body
2.	R	q	Sd	
3.	L	q	Cl	
4.	R	S	Bwd (LTn)	RH Palm
5.	L	q	Sd	
6.	R	q	Cl	

Woman's Part

	Foot	Rhythm	Direction
1.	R	S	Bwd (LTn)
2.	L	q	Sd
3.	R	q	Cl
4.	L	S	Fwd (LTn)
5.	R	q	Sd
6.	L	q	Cl

Teaching Hints

At the completion of these six steps, beginners will have executed a 90° turn while advanced dancers will have executed a 180° turn.

ARCH TRAVEL

Position—Closed to Arch to Closed

Man's Part

	Foot	Rhythm	Direction	Lead
1.	L	S	Fwd	LH High
2.	R	q	Sd	RH Palm
3.	L	q	Cl	
4.	R	S	Fwd	Body
5.	L	q	Sd	
6.	R	q	Cl	

Woman's Part

	Foot	Rhythm	Direction
1.	R	S	Fwd (RTn)
2.	L	q	Sd
3.	R	q	Cl
4.	L	S	Bwd
5.	R	q	Sd
6.	L	q	Cl

Teaching Hints

Dancers must remember to stay directly in front of each other when executing the turn. On step 1 the woman must execute a 360° turn while turning under the arch.

CHASSÉ

Position—Closed

Man's Part

	Foot	Rhythm	Direction	Lead
1.	L	S	Sd	RH Palm
2.	R	q	Cl	
3.	L	q	Sd	
4.	R	S	Cl	
5.	L	q	Sd	
6.	R	q	Cl	

Woman's Part

	Foot	Rhythm	Direction
1.	R	S	Sd
2.	L	q	Cl
3.	R	q	Sd
4.	L	S	Cl
5.	R	q	Sd
6.	L	q	Cl

Teaching Hints

Chassé steps move continually sideward to either the left or right and may be danced in the basic rhythm or in all quick steps. The Chassé may be initiated with a forward (L) slow step and six Chassés to the man's right, followed by the backward half of the Rumba Basic. It may also be executed starting with a backward slow(R) step and six Chassés to the man's left.

BACK CROSS

Position—Closed to Reverse to Closed

Man's Part

	Foot	Rhythm	Direction	Lead
1.	L	S	Fwd	Body
2.	R	q	Sd	
3.	L	q	Cl	
4.	R	S	BwdX	RH Fingertips
5.	L	q	Sd	
6.	R	q	Cl	

Woman's Part

	Foot	Rhythm	Direction
1.	R	S	Bwd
2.	L	q	Sd
3.	R	q	Cl
4.	L	S	BwdX
5.	R	q	Sd
6.	L	q	Cl

Teaching Hints

This step begins with the first half of the Rumba Basic. Dancers should assume the Reverse Position on the Backward Cross, step 4, and immediately return to the Closed Position on step 5.

FRONT CROSS

Position—Closed to Semi-Open

Man's Part

	Foot	Rhythm	Direction	Lead
1.	L	S	Fwd	Body
2.	R	q	Sd	
3.	L	q	Cl	
4.	R	S	Bwd	RH Palm
5.	L	q	Sd	
6.	R	q	FwdX	RH Heel

Woman's Part

	Foot	Rhythm	Direction
1.	R	S	Bwd
2.	L	q	Sd
3.	R	q	Cl
4.	L	S	Fwd
5.	R	q	Sd
6.	L	q	Fwd X

Teaching Hints

This step leaves the dancers in Semi-Open Position. A strong right-hand fingertip lead after the forward cross brings dancers back to Closed Position.

REVERSE WHEEL

Position—Closed to Right Side

Man's Part

	Foot	Rhythm	Direction	Lead
1.	L	S	BwdX (LTn)	RH Palm
2.	R	q	Bwd	
3.	L	q	Bwd	
4.	R	S	Bwd	
5.	L	q	Bwd	
6.	R	q	Bwd	

Woman's Part

	Foot	Rhythm	Direction
1.	R	S	Bwd (LTn)
2.	L	q	Bwd
3.	R	q	Bwd
4.	L	S	Bwd
5.	R	q	Bwd
6.	L	q	Bwd

Teaching Hints

The backward movement of this step is initiated by the slight left turn of the man's body. As this happens, his right shoulder and right-hand lead must be strong to indicate the woman's backward movement. Both partners turn slightly left on step 1 to assume the Right Side Position. For added style, partners should look at each other while turning.

SIDE BREAK

Position—Closed to Open

Man's Part

	Foot	Rhythm	Direction	Lead
1.	L	S	Sd	
2.	R	q	BwdX (RTn)	RH Fingertips
3.	L	q	IP	
4.	R	S	Sd	
5.	L	q	BwdX (LTn)	LH Push
6.	R	q	IP	

Woman's Part

	Foot	Rhythm	Direction
1.	R	S	Sd
2.	L	q	BwdX (LTn)
3.	R	q	IP
4.	L	S	Sd
5.	R	q	BwdX (RTn)
6.	L	q	IP

Teaching Hints

Students should practice the Side Break by dancing it immediately following the forward half of the Rumba Basic. On steps 2 and 5 the dancers swing into Open Position (90° turn) and return to Closed Position on step 3.

BEGINNING ROUTINES

ROUTINE ONE

1. Rumba Basic
2. Rumba Basic
3. Left Turn
4. Left Turn
5. Arch Travel
6. Arch Travel
7. Repeat

ROUTINE TWO

1. Rumba Basic
2. Arch Travel
3. Chasse
4. Rumba Basic
5. Back Cross
6. Back Cross
7. Left Turn
8. Repeat

ROUTINE THREE

1. Rumba Basic
2. Back Cross
3. Back Cross
4. Arch Travel
5. Front Cross
6. Front Cross
7. Arch Travel
8. Repeat

ROUTINE FOUR

1. Rumba Basic
2. Chasse
3. Rumba Basic
4. Reverse Wheel
5. Front Cross
6. Back Cross
7. Repeat

ADVANCED SECTION

BOLERO BREAK

Position—Closed to Sweetheart

Man's Part

	Foot	Rhythm	Direction	Lead
1.	L	S	Fwd	LH High
2.	R	q	Sd	
3.	L	q	Cl	
4.	R	S	Fwd	
5.	L	q	Sd	
6.	R	q	Cl	
7.	L	S	Bwd	RH Pull
8.	R	q	Sd	
9.	L	q	Cl	
10.	R	S	Bwd	
11.	L	q	Sd	
12.	R	q	Cl	

Bolero Break

Woman's Part

	Foot	Rhythm	Direction
1.	R	S	Fwd (RTn)
2.	L	q	Fwd
3.	R	q	Cl
4.	L	S	Fwd
5.	R	q	Fwd
6.	L	q	Cl
7.	R	S	Fwd (LTn)
8.	L	q	Bwd
9.	R	q	Cl
10.	L	S	Bwd
11.	R	q	Sd
12.	L	q	Cl

Bolero Break

Teaching Hints

As shown above, the man executes two forward Rumba steps as he circles the woman clockwise under his left arm in a large arc (steps 1-6). Dancers grasp right hands in step 7 in preparation for the Sweetheart Position in which they end. (See photographs.)

Bolero Break

Wrap

Wrap

WRAP

Position—Two Hands to Wrap

Man's Part

	Foot	Rhythm	Direction	Lead
1.	L	S	Fwd	Body
2.	R	q	Sd	LH Push
3.	L	q	Cl	
4.	R	S	Bwd	LH High
5.	L	q	Sd	RH Palm
6.	R	q	Cl	

Woman's Part

	Foot	Rhythm	Direction
1.	R	S	Bwd
2.	L	q	Sd
3.	R	q	Cl
4.	L	S	Fwd (LTn)
5.	R	q	Bwd
6.	L	q	Cl

Teaching Hints

On step 4 the slight pulling action of the man's left hand with the raising of his left arm gives the woman her directional cue. Step 4 is a 180° turn for the woman. (See photographs.)

UNWRAP

Position—Sweetheart to Closed

Man's Part

	Foot	Rhythm	Direction	Lead
1.	L	S	Fwd	LH High
2.	R	q	Sd	RH Push
3.	L	q	Cl	
4.	R	S	Bwd	LH Pull
5.	L	q	Sd	
6.	R	q	Cl	

Woman's Part

	Foot	Rhythm	Direction
1.	R	S	Fwd (RTn)
2.	L	q	Bwd
3.	R	q	Cl
4.	L	S	Fwd
5.	R	q	Sd
6.	L	q	Cl

Teaching Hints

Frequently, the Unwrap is also used when coming out of the Wrap Position. Step 1 for the woman is a 180° turn. (See photographs.)

Unwrap   Unwrap   Unwrap

OPEN WALK TURN

Position—Open

Man's Part

	Foot	Rhythm	Direction	Lead
1.	L	S	Fwd	RH Palm
2.	R	q	Sd	
3.	L	q	Cl	
4.	R	S	Fwd	RH Heel
5.	L	q	Sd	
6.	R	q	Cl	

Woman's Part

	Foot	Rhythm	Direction
1.	R	S	Fwd
2.	L	q	Sd
3.	R	q	Cl
4.	L	S	Fwd (RTn)
5.	R	q	Bwd (RTn)
6.	L	q	Cl

Teaching Hints

For the woman, steps 4 and 5 are 180° turns in the line of direction. To return to a Closed Position, partners must turn into each other on the first slow of the next figure. It is also possible for the woman to do left turns on steps 4 and 5.

BREAK AWAY

Position—Closed to Full Open

Man's Part

	Foot	Rhythm	Direction	Lead
1.	L	S	Fwd (LTn)	RH Heel
2.	R	q	Fwd (LTn)	
3.	L	q	Cl	
4.	R	S	Fwd	
5.	L	q	Sd	
6.	R	q	Cl	

Woman's Part

	Foot	Rhythm	Direction
1.	R	S	Fwd (RTn)
2.	L	q	Fwd (RTn)
3.	R	q	Cl
4.	L	S	Fwd
5.	R	q	Sd
6.	L	q	Cl

Break Away

Break Away

Teaching Hints

The man leads the 180° turns by releasing the joined hands and immediately applying pressure on his partner's back with the heel of his right hand. In steps 1 and 2, dancers turn away from each other in a small circle. They move toward each other in step 4 to resume a Closed Position and complete the "side, close." The Break Away may be cued by saying, "Turn-2-3, Forward-Side-Close." (See photographs.)

ROCK

Position—Closed

Man's Part

	Foot	Rhythm	Direction	Lead
1.	L	S	Fwd	Body
2.	R	q	Fwd	
3.	L	q	Bwd	RH Palm Body
4.	R	S	Fwd	
5.	L	q	Fwd	
6.	R	q	Bwd	RH Palm

Woman's Part

	Foot	Rhythm	Direction
1.	R	S	Bwd
2.	L	q	Bwd
3.	R	q	Fwd
4.	L	S	Bwd
5.	R	q	Bwd
6.	L	q	Fwd

Teaching Hints

The Rock may also begin with the man moving backward and the woman moving forward. This step also looks stylish when executed in Open Position.

ADVANCED ROUTINES

ROUTINE ONE

1. Bolero Break
2. Open Walk Turn
3. Open Walk Turn (to Closed Position)
4. Rock
5. Rock
6. Break Away
7. Repeat

ROUTINE TWO

1. Rock
2. Rock
3. Wrap
4. Unwrap
5. Open Walk Turn
6. Open Walk Turn
7. Break Away
8. Repeat

ROUTINE THREE

1. Bolero Break
2. Rock
3. Bolero Break
4. Break Away
5. Wrap
6. Unwrap
7. Repeat

ROUTINE FOUR

1. Wrap
2. Unwrap
3. Break Away
4. Open Walk Turn
5. Break Away
6. Rock
7. Bolero Break
8. Repeat

9

the samba

Although classified as a Latin American dance, the Samba originated among the African natives who were uprooted and brought to Brazil during its colonization period. During periodic religious festivals the Afro-Brazilians celebrated by dancing to the scintillating rhythms of their unique, percussive instruments. Attracted to this exciting rhythm, Brazilian socialites modified the free and exuberant Samba for the ballroom during the 1920s.

In 1935 the Samba was introduced into the United States where it failed to gain wide popularity because few musicians were acquainted with the Brazilian percussive instruments that created the sound and mood of the Samba. Today, while it continues to be the popular festive dance in Brazil, the Samba has become one of America's more popular ballroom dance forms because it invites uninhibited expression to its irresistible sound.

TEMPO

The Samba is danced to a wide range of tempos. Beginners favor a tempo of 120 beats per minute while advanced dancers generally prefer a lively tempo of around 140 beats per minute.

RHYTHM

The Samba is danced to music written in 2/4 time with the accent on the second beat of each measure. Rhythmically, the basic step and the Copacabana step are danced in a combination of two quick steps and one slow step (qqS). Another popular rhythm, the Brazilian, is danced in a combination of six quick steps and one slow step (qqqqqqS). The music notations for these two rhythms are as follows:

qqS Rhythm

2/4	♪♪♩ ♪♪♩
Count	1 & 2 1 & 2
Rhythm	q q S q q S

qqqqqqS Rhythm

2/4	♪♪♪♪♪♪♩ ♪♪♩ ♩ ♩ ♩
Count	1 & 2 & 3 & 4 1 & 2& 3& 4
Rhythm	q q q q q q S q q qq qq S

STEPS

The following steps are included in this chapter:

Beginner's Section: Samba Basic, Left Turn, Right Turn, Side Break, Wheel, Balance, Arch, and Crossover

Advanced Section: qqS Rhythm—Copacabana Walk, Copacabana Semi-Open Walk, Swivel, Double Arch and Break Away

qqqqqqS Rhythm—Cross Chassé, Advanced Left Turn, Advanced Right Turn

STYLING

The Samba has a conspicuously distinct style that is often described as resembling a swinging pendulum. Although danced to a lively beat, the basic step of the Samba is a smooth, swaying dance characterized by an easily noticeable rise and fall. During this dance the body remains erect and relaxed with the head held high and relatively still as the feet move forward and backward, allowing the man and woman to dance alternately under each other.

The basic step, danced in qqS rhythm, is performed with a flat-footed first step, followed by a second step on the ball of the foot, and concluded with a flat-footed third step. This footwork, combined with a straightening and relaxing of the knees, produces the attractive rise and fall of the Samba.

The Copacabana step is somewhat more difficult to dance and has a distinct movement. This step, also danced in qqS rhythm with three changes of weight, differs from the basic step in that the basic may be described as step, close, in-place, whereas the Copacabana is a step, in-place, in-place. As the dancers complete the second in-place, they should draw the foot backward with a slight kicking action before beginning the next Copacabana dance step. This combination of foot movements gives a rocking appearance to this attractive traveling step.

The most intriguing rhythm of the Samba is the Brazilian rhythm (qqqqqqS). Because of the series of six quick steps, this rhythm must be danced in very small steps that express the music as the upper body remains relaxed but relatively quiet. The Brazilian step exemplifies the light and lively movement of the intriguing Samba.

TEACHING THE SAMBA

Sometimes referred to as the Latin American Polka, the Samba is an exacting dance form. Its distinct beat is easy to follow once the basic dance patterns are mastered.

The Samba includes an attractive combination of spot steps danced in the basic rhythm and traveling steps danced in the Copacabana rhythm. Unlike the Fox-Trot and Waltz where dancers travel throughout the dance floor in the line of dance (LOD), the Samba is more confined to circular traveling steps in a smaller area. Consequently, teachers may encounter some difficulty in organizing their students for group instruction.

For the steps in the basic rhythm, a space of ten square feet for each couple is sufficient. When teaching the step in the Copacabana rhythm, the couples should be arranged so that they can travel together back and forth across the ballroom floor.

Initially, instruction should focus on the unique style of the basic rhythm. The pendulum-like motion is captured by keeping the head and upper body rather stationary as the feet and lower body move back and forth, emphasizing an elongated first step of each quick-quick-slow pattern. After the students begin to move in the basic rhythm, they will learn the steps rather quickly.

Because of their similarity, the basic rhythm is a good introduction to the Copacabana rhythm; however, considerable time and attention should be given to the Copacabana's unique foot pattern. The Copacabana is performed basically in a step-close-step pattern with the "close" entailing a closing of the feet to a toe to heel position. At the conclusion of each step-close-step pattern, the dancers should draw (kick) the trailing foot backward before beginning the next step-close-step pattern. Since beginning dancers frequently have difficulty learning this rhythm, it may be advisable to employ a follow-the-leader or Bunny Hop teaching method before organizing the class in couples.

In addition to the rhythmic, directional, and foot cues, the teacher should employ descriptive cues that sharpen the focus of the dancers on the style and rhythm of the Samba. Cues, such as Long-Short-Short and Step-Close-

Step-Kick, are very helpful in teaching the basic and Copacabana rhythms respectively. The cue Flat-Up-Up reminds the students to emphasize the rise and fall characteristic of the basic rhythm. Although some students may encounter some initial difficulty with styling, all will enjoy the delightfully expressive rhythm of the Samba.

BEGINNING SECTION

SAMBA BASIC

Position—Closed

Man's Part

	Foot	Rhythm	Direction	Lead
1.	L	q	Fwd	Body
2.	R	q	Cl	
3.	L	S	IP	
4.	R	q	Bwd	RH Palm
5.	L	q	Cl	
6.	R	S	IP	

Woman's Part

	Foot	Rhythm	Direction
1.	R	q	Bwd
2.	L	q	Cl
3.	R	S	IP
4.	L	q	Fwd
5.	R	q	Cl
6.	L	S	IP

Samba Basic

Samba Basic

Teaching Hints

The Samba Basic is a spot step and the foundation upon which all the other steps are built. Considerable time should be given to this step so that the dancers can learn the unique, pendulum-like movement of the Samba. The dancers should remember to keep their heads still and erect as their feet move forward and backward. (See photographs.)

LEFT TURN

Position—Closed

Man's Part

	Foot	Rhythm	Direction	Lead
1.	L	q	Fwd (LTn)	Body
2.	R	q	Cl	
3.	L	S	IP	
4.	R	q	Bwd (LTn)	RH Palm
5.	L	q	Cl	
6.	R	S	IP	

Woman's Part

	Foot	Rhythm	Direction
1.	R	q	Bwd (LTn)
2.	L	q	Cl
3.	R	S	IP
4.	L	q	Fwd (LTn)
5.	R	q	Cl
6.	L	S	IP

Teaching Hints

This step is very easy to learn once the basic rhythm is mastered. The turn occurs during the entire pattern, although the lead is strongest during the first and fourth steps when body sway to the left is quite pronounced.

RIGHT TURN

Position—Closed

Man's Part

	Foot	Rhythm	Direction	Lead
1.	L	q	Bwd (RTn)	RH Heel
2.	R	q	Cl	
3.	L	S	IP	
4.	R	q	Fwd (RTn)	Body
5.	L	q	Cl	
6.	R	S	IP	

Woman's Part

	Foot	Rhythm	Direction
1.	R	q	Fwd (RTn)
2.	L	q	Cl
3.	R	S	IP
4.	L	q	Bwd (RTn)
5.	R	q	Cl
6.	L	S	IP

Teaching Hints

Sometimes a difficult step, the Right Turn may require a very detailed step-by-step breakdown. Although it may be taught as described above, some students learn this step more readily if they dance forward into the turn by using the first half of the Samba Basic and then proceeding into the Right Turn with step 4. The turn occurs throughout the six steps, with the leads given on the first and fourth steps when body sway is most pronounced. The forward and backward steps are actually diagonal in direction.

SIDE BREAK

Position—Closed to Reverse to Semi-Open

Man's Part

	Foot	*Rhythm*	*Direction*	*Lead*
1.	L	q	Sd	
2.	R	q	Bwd X	RH Fingertips
3.	L	S	IP	
4.	R	q	Sd	
5.	L	q	Bwd X	RH Palm
6.	R	S	IP	

Woman's Part

	Foot	*Rhythm*	*Direction*
1.	R	q	Sd
2.	L	q	Bwd X
3.	R	S	IP
4.	L	q	Sd
5.	R	q	Bwd X
6.	L	S	IP

Teaching Hints

This flirtatious step entails alternately opening into Reverse and Semi-Open Positions. The dancers may, if they wish, break to a Full Open instead of Semi-Open Position. All steps must be small to assure timely changes of position.

WHEEL

Position—Right Side

Man's Part

	Foot	*Rhythm*	*Direction*	*Lead*
1.	L	q	Fwd	RH Palm
2.	R	q	Cl	
3.	L	S	IP	
4.	R	q	Fwd	
5.	L	q	Cl	
6.	R	S	IP	

Woman's Part

	Foot	*Rhythm*	*Direction*
1.	R	q	Fwd
2.	L	q	Cl
3.	R	S	IP
4.	L	q	Fwd
5.	R	q	Cl
6.	L	S	IP

Teaching Hints

The footwork of this step appears easy to learn; however, since both dancers are moving forward, the basic dance movement is replaced by the Copacabana step (see the section on styling in the beginning of this chapter). Before introducing the Wheel, instructors should teach the foot pattern of the Copacabana.

BALANCE

Position—Closed

Man's Part

	Foot	Rhythm	Direction	Lead
1.	L	q	Fwd	Body
2.	R	q	Tc	RH Lift
3.	L	S	Ho	
4.	R	q	Bwd	RH Palm
5.	L	q	Tc	RH Lift
6.	R	S	Ho	

Woman's Part

	Foot	Rhythm	Direction
1.	R	q	Bwd
2.	L	q	Tc
3.	R	S	Ho
4.	L	q	Fwd
5.	R	q	Tc
6.	L	S	Ho

Teaching Hints

The movement of the Balance is simply a step followed by a touch of the non-supporting foot to the heel of the supporting foot. In addition to the upper body and palm leads, the man must "lift" slightly with his right hand so that his partner will distinguish the Balance from the Samba Basic.

ARCH

Position—Semi-Open

Man's Part

	Foot	Rhythm	Direction	Lead
1.	L	q	Fwd	LH High
2.	R	q	Cl	RH Palm
3.	L	S	IP	
4.	R	q	Fwd	
5.	L	q	Cl	
6.	R	S	IP	

Woman's Part

	Foot	Rhythm	Direction
1.	R	q	Fwd (RTn)
2.	L	q	IP
3.	R	S	IP
4.	L	q	Bwd
5.	R	q	IP
6.	L	S	IP

Teaching Hints

During the Arch the man performs the Samba Basic, while the woman, using the Copacabana step, turns clockwise under the arch formed by the man's left and the woman's right hand. The woman must refrain from hurrying through the 360° turn, which may take an additional six steps to complete smoothly. Although the raised left hand is the primary lead, a palm lead is helpful in directing the woman under the arch.

CROSSOVER

Position—Closed to Semi-Open to Closed

Man's Part

	Foot	Rhythm	Direction	Lead
1.	L	q	Fwd	Body
2.	R	q	Cl	
3.	L	S	IP	
4.	R	q	FwdX	RH Heel
5.	L	q	Sd	
6.	R	S	IP	

Woman's Part

	Foot	Rhythm	Direction
1.	R	q	Bwd
2.	L	q	Cl
3.	R	S	IP
4.	L	q	Fwd X
5.	R	q	Sd
6.	L	S	IP

Teaching Hints

Although this step is quite simple, it is difficult to execute at fast tempos. It requires sharp, timely leads that move the dancers from one dance position to another. The dancers may stay in the Semi-Open Position and continue with dance steps using the Copacabana foot pattern rather than returning to the Closed Position.

BEGINNING ROUTINES

The following routines employ the basic and the Copacabana dance patterns of the Samba. The first two routines, however, consist of steps danced only in the basic dance pattern.

ROUTINE ONE

1. Samba Basic
2. Samba Basic
3. Side Break
4. Side Break
5. Left Turn
6. Left Turn
7. Repeat in reverse direction

ROUTINE TWO

1. Samba Basic
2. Samba Basic
3. Right Turn
4. Right Turn
5. Left Turn
6. Left Turn
7. Repeat

ROUTINE THREE

1. Samba Basic
2. Samba Basic
3. Wheel
4. Wheel
5. Balance
6. Balance
7. Arch
8. Repeat

ROUTINE FOUR

1. Samba Basic
2. Samba Basic
3. Crossover
4. Left Turn
5. Left Turn
6. Balance
7. Repeat in reverse direction

ADVANCED SECTION

The Samba steps included in this section are written in two rhythms—the basic (qqS) and the Brazilian (qqqqqqS). The steps in basic rhythm are danced in the Copacabana foot pattern, while the Brazilian rhythm is danced in very small steps using a step-close pattern. Mastery of these steps will give the dancers a variety of steps that combine beautifully into attractive enjoyable routines.

COPACABANA WALK

Position—Closed

Man's Part

	Foot	Rhythm	Direction	Lead
1.	L	q	Fwd	Body
2.	R	q	Cl	RH Palm
3.	L	S	IP	
4.	R	q	Fwd	Body
5.	L	q	Cl	RH Palm
6.	R	S	IP	

Woman's Part

	Foot	Rhythm	Direction
1.	R	q	Bwd
2.	L	q	Cl
3.	R	S	IP
4.	L	q	Bwd
5.	R	q	Cl
6.	L	S	IP

Teaching Hints

This step has a few subtleties that must be demonstrated clearly. When the dancers take the second and fifth steps, they "close" to a toe-to-heel position rather than a side-by-side. And, when the man takes his in-place step, he should kick his foot back slightly to create and maintain the rocking motion characteristic of the Copacabana. This step can also be danced in the reverse direction with the man moving backward and his partner forward. When dancing backward, the dancers will be unable to add the slight kicking action of the Copacabana step.

COPACABANA SEMI-OPEN WALK

Position—Semi-Open

Man's Part

	Foot	Rhythm	Direction	Lead
1.	L	q	Fwd	RH Palm
2.	R	q	Cl	
3.	L	S	IP	
4.	R	q	Fwd	RH Palm
5.	L	q	Cl	
6.	R	S	IP	

Woman's Part

	Foot	Rhythm	Direction
1.	R	q	Fwd
2.	L	q	Cl
3.	R	S	IP
4.	L	q	Fwd
5.	R	q	Cl
6.	L	S	IP

Copacabana Semi-Open Walk

Teaching Hints

This step is relatively easy for students to learn since the man and the woman employ identical footwork. Here also, the dancers "close" to a toe-to-heel position in steps 2 and 5 and draw the foot back slightly on the in-place movement. This step flows beautifully out of the Cross Step. (See photograph.)

SWIVEL

Position—One Hand (R to L)

Man's Part

	Foot	Rhythm	Direction	Lead
1.	L	q	Fwd (LTn)	RH Push
2.	R	q	IP	
3.	L	S	IP	
4.	R	q	Fwd (RTn)	RH Pull
5.	L	q	IP	
6.	R	S	IP	

Woman's Part

	Foot	Rhythm	Direction
1.	R	q	Fwd (RTn)
2.	L	q	IP
3.	R	S	IP
4.	L	q	Fwd (LTn)
5.	R	q	IP
6.	L	S	IP

Swivel

Teaching Hints

Basically, this step consists of partners alternately turning away and toward each other using the Copacabana foot pattern. The forward steps are made diagonally, resulting in a swivel-like movement as the partners move away from and then toward each other. The right-hand lead is a pushing and pulling action. This step may also be done in the Open Position. (See photographs.)

Swivel

DOUBLE ARCH

Position—Semi-Open to Back-to-Back to Semi-Open

Man's Part

	Foot	Rhythm	Direction	Lead
1.	L	q	Fwd (LTn)	LH High
2.	R	q	IP	
3.	L	S	IP	
4.	R	q	Bwd (LTn)	
5.	L	q	IP	
6.	R	S	IP	

Woman's Part

	Foot	Rhythm	Direction
1.	R	q	Fwd (RTn)
2.	L	q	IP
3.	R	S	IP
4.	L	q	Bwd (RTn)
5.	R	q	IP
6.	L	S	IP

Teaching Hints

This step demands that both dancers turn 360° and use the Copacabana footwork as they pass under the arch formed by the man's left and woman's right hand. The lead consists of a raised left hand accompanied by pressure from the right palm. Beginning dancers may find it more comfortable to complete this step and return to the Semi-Open Position by employing an additional six steps.

BREAK AWAY

Position—One Hand (R to L) to Free

Man's Part

	Foot	Rhythm	Direction	Lead
1.	L	q	Fwd (LTn)	RH Push
2.	R	q	IP	
3.	L	S	IP	
4.	R	q	Fwd (LTn)	
5.	L	q	IP	
6.	R	S	IP	

Break Away

Woman's Part

	Foot	Rhythm	Direction
1.	R	q	Fwd (RTn)
2.	L	q	IP
3.	R	S	IP
4.	L	q	Fwd (RTn)
5.	R	q	IP
6.	L	S	IP

Teaching Hints

This step consists of both dancers turning away from each other and then circling back to each other, using the Copacabana footwork throughout. The dancers should refrain from hurrying through this step and should take six additional steps if necessary to complete it smoothly. The man should lead into this step from a Semi-Open Walk or a Swivel. The right-hand lead is a push of the woman's left hand to her right. (See photographs.)

Break Away

CROSS CHASSÉ

Position—Closed

Man's Part

	Foot	Rhythm	Direction	Lead
1.	L	q	FwdX	RH Fingertips
2.	R	q	Cl	RH Palm
3.	L	q	FwdX	
4.	R	q	Cl	
5.	L	q	FwdX	
6.	R	q	Cl	
7.	L	S	FwdX	

Woman's Part

	Foot	Rhythm	Direction
1.	R	q	Fwd X
2.	L	q	Cl
3.	R	q	Fwd X
4.	L	q	Cl
5.	R	q	Fwd X
6.	L	q	Cl
7.	R	S	Fwd X

Teaching Hints

This step is a combination of a forward cross and a chassé performed in a cross-legged position. After crossing one foot over the other, the dancers simply "close" the non-supporting foot next to the supporting foot keeping a cross-legged position. The above step is danced to the man's right. A second Cross Chassé would be danced to his left by crossing the free foot (his right, her left) and repeating this step to the left.

ADVANCED LEFT TURN

Position—Closed

Man's Part

	Foot	Rhythm	Direction	Lead
1.	L	q	Fwd (LTn)	RH Fingertips
2.	R	q	Cl	
3.	L	q	IP (LTn)	
4.	R	q	Cl	
5.	L	q	IP (LTn)	
6.	R	q	Cl	
7.	L	S	IP (LTn)	

Woman's Part

	Foot	Rhythm	Direction
1.	R	q	Bwd (LTn)
2.	L	q	Cl
3.	R	q	Bwd (LTn)
4.	L	q	Cl
5.	R	q	Bwd (LTn)
6.	L	q	Cl
7.	R	S	Bwd (LTn)

Teaching Hints

The man's part is basically a turning in place on the left foot and a closing of the right foot to a toe-to-heel position; the woman's footwork consists of stepping backward and turning left on the right foot and closing the left foot to a heel-to-toe position. This 180° turn is performed with body sway to the left throughout the turn. The man should lead out of this turn with the backward half of the Samba Basic.

ADVANCED RIGHT TURN

Position—Closed

Man's Part

	Foot	Rhythm	Direction	Lead
1.	R	q	Fwd (RTn)	RH Heel
2.	L	q	Cl	
3.	R	q	IP (RTn)	
4.	L	q	Cl	
5.	R	q	IP (RTn)	
6.	L	q	Cl	
7.	R	S	IP (RTn)	

Woman's Part

	Foot	Rhythm	Direction
1...	L	q	Bwd (RTn)
2.	R	q	Cl
3.	L	q	Bwd (RTn)
4.	R	q	Cl
5.	L	q	Bwd (RTn)
6.	R	q	Cl
7.	L	S	Bwd (RTn)

Teaching Hints

This 180° turn begins on the man's right and the woman's left foot. Therefore, the man should lead into the turn from the forward half of the Samba Basic. The man's footwork essentially consists of turning in place on his right foot and closing his left foot to a toe-to-heel position. The woman's part consists of stepping backward and turning on the left foot and closing her right foot to a heel-to-toe position. Body sway to the right occurs throughout the turn. The man should lead out of this step with a Samba Basic.

ADVANCED ROUTINES

These advanced routines include basic steps and advanced steps and require limited space for each couple.

ROUTINE ONE

1. Samba Basic
2. Samba Basic
3. Copacabana Walk
4. Copacabana Walk
5. Copacabana Semi-Open Walk
6. Copacabana Semi-Open Walk
7. Double Arch
8. Repeat

ROUTINE TWO

1. Copacabana Walk
2. Copacabana Walk
3. Copacabana Semi-Open Walk
4. Copacabana Semi-Open Walk
5. Swivel
6. Swivel
7. Break Away
8. Repeat

ROUTINE THREE

1. Samba Basic
2. Samba Basic
3. Cross Chassé (R)
4. Cross Chassé (L)
5. Samba Basic
6. Samba Basic
7. Advanced Left Turn (180°)
8. Advanced Right Turn (180°)
9. Repeat

ROUTINE FOUR

1. Copacabana Walk
2. Copacabana Walk
3. Samba Basic
4. Cross Chassé (R)
5. Samba Basic (Backward half)
6. Advanced Left Turn (180°)
7. Samba Basic (Backward half)
8. Repeat in reverse direction

10

the tango

The Tango originated in Spain where it was performed by a solo dancer. The staccato 2/4 rhythm was accented by fancy heel rhythms, snapping fingers, and graceful arm movements.

The social form of the Tango as it is known today was originated by the gauchos in Argentina in the 1880s. Originally the dance was called "El Baile con Corté," meaning "the dance with a stop."

In 1910 this Argentine dance was introduced in Europe where it regained its Spanish name but underwent many changes in steps and styling. By 1913, it had reached the United States where Irene and Vernon Castle brought it back to its original Argentine styling and rhythm.

TEMPO

The Tango is usually danced in either a slow or medium tempo to maintain its beautiful, sophisticated style. It is advisable to begin with a slow tempo for beginners until the steps and timing are coordinated. About 128 beats per minute are comfortable for the beginner while the advanced dancer usually likes a slightly faster tempo of 140 beats per minute.

RHYTHM

Tango music is written in 2/4 and 4/4 time with beginners preferring the 4/4 rhythm because it is slower and easier to follow. Each completed Tango step requires eight beats that take two measures in 4/4 time. This is written as follows:

4/4	♩	♩	♩ ♩ ♩	♩	♩	♩ ♩ ♩
Count	1-2	3-4	5 6 7-8	1-2	3-4	5 6 7-8
Rhythm	S	S	q q S	S	S	q q S

STEPS

Those steps to be included for the Tango are:

Beginner's Section: SSqqS—Tango Basic, Basic Corté, Travel, Arch Turn, Crossover, Right Turn, Left Turn

SSqq—Argentine Walk

Advanced Section: SSqqS—Advanced Travel, Corté Left Turn, The Fascination

qqSSqq—Advanced Corté, Fan

STYLING

Erect posture and a good sense of balance are essential for the controlled, inviting style of the Tango. Dancers should not lean on each other for support. Each step is kept close to the floor and originates from the hips. The *slows* are long steps while the *quicks* are short steps. The quick steps are both sharp and on the beat, thus the contrast between the slow and quick steps gives the Tango its unmistakable style. Refer to chapter 2 for any further styling techniques.

TEACHING THE TANGO

The beginner should master the Walk individually, both forward and backward, before moving into a Closed Position. Dancers should be encouraged to explore changes of direction and position without changing the basic Walk, such as walking in small circles both clockwise and counterclockwise and (in partners) moving both forward and backward in a Semi-Open Position. The walk is written as follows:

THE WALK

Position—Closed

Man's Part

	Foot	Rhythm	Direction	Lead
1.	L	S	Fwd	Body
2.	R	S	Fwd	
3.	L	q	Fwd	
4.	R	q	Fwd	
5.	L	S	Fwd	

Woman's Part

	Foot	Rhythm	Direction
1.	R	S	Bwd
2.	L	S	Bwd
3.	R	q	Bwd
4.	L	q	Bwd
5.	R	S	Bwd

Erect, but not stiff, posture is important in performing the Walk since this allows the steps to easily flow from the hips rather than the knees. If the beginner is still bouncing the steps, he or she should be reminded of the long, slow steps and short, quick steps. Raising the feet too far off the ground is also a problem for beginners. To correct this, they should be reminded that the feet are kept close to the floor, much like normal walking steps. Dancers showing proficiency should try to sustain the slow steps as long as possible before shifting their weight to the next steps.

When practicing the Corté, beginners commonly keep so low that they cannot recover on the proper beat. To help eliminate this, the teacher should have the dancers turn out the supporting foot which will act as a brake. To perform the Corté smoothly takes practice and control.

These are a number of verbal cues that are helpful when teaching the Tango: Slow-Slow-quick-quick-Slow, Slow-Slow-quick-quick-Draw(or Touch), or 1-2, 3-4, 5, 6, 7-8. Teachers must be thoroughly familiar with the music they have chosen to effectively use the verbal cues. Before class, teachers should practice the cuing by playing the music and talking through the cues.

BEGINNING SECTION

TANGO BASIC

Position—Closed

Man's Part

	Foot	Rhythm	Direction	Lead
1.	L	S	Fwd	Body
2.	R	S	Fwd	
3.	L	q	Sd	RH Palm
4.	R	q	Cl	
5.	L	S	Fwd	

Woman's Part

	Foot	Rhythm	Direction
1.	R	S	Bwd
2.	L	S	Bwd
3.	R	q	Sd
4.	L	q	Cl
5.	R	S	Bwd

Tango Basic

125

Teaching Hints

This step may also be executed moving backward for the man and forward for the woman. It develops into a turning figure when quarter turns are inserted on the slow steps. The slow steps are long reaching steps. (See photograph.)

BASIC CORTÉ

Position—Closed

Basic Corté

Man's Part

	Foot	Rhythm	Direction	Lead
1.	L	S	Bwd	RH Palm
2.	R	S	Fwd	Body
3.	L	q	Fwd	Body
4.	R	q	Sd	RH Palm
5.	L	S	Dr	

Woman's Part

	Foot	Rhythm	Direction
1.	R	S	Fwd
2.	L	S	Bwd
3.	R	q	Bwd
4.	L	q	Sd
5.	R	S	Dr

Teaching Hints

The Corté, or stop, can be executed on any two slow steps. As the man steps backward, his left knee must be relaxed, leaving his right foot in place. He recovers by shifting his weight forward to the right foot and finishes the step with a quick, quick, slow moving forward. This final quick, quick, slow, or Fwd-Sd-Cl, is sometimes called "The Tango Close." Another way to verbally cue this step is to say "Corté(S)-Recover(S)-Tango(q,q)-Close(S). (See photographs.)

TRAVEL

Position—Closed

Draw (Tango)

Man's Part

	Foot	Rhythm	Direction	Lead
1.	L	S	Fwd	Body
2.	R	S	Fwd	
3.	L	q	Fwd	
4.	R	q	Sd	LH Palm
5.	L	S	Tc	

Woman's Part

	Foot	Rhythm	Direction
1.	R	S	Bwd
2.	L	S	Bwd
3.	R	q	Bwd
4.	L	q	Sd
5.	R	S	Tc

Teaching Hints

The important point to remember on the Travel is that the touch in step 5 must not assume any weight. This will cause the step to begin with the same foot on each repetition. Note that whenever the combination of Fwd-Sd-Tc appears in a figure it is called a "Tango Close."

ARCH TURN

Position—Closed

Man's Part

	Foot	Rhythm	Direction	Lead
1.	L	S	Fwd	LH High
2.	R	S	Fwd	RH Palm
3.	L	q	Fwd	
4.	R	q	Sd	RH Palm
5.	L	S	Dr	

Woman's Part

	Foot	Rhythm	Direction
1.	R	S	Fwd (RTn)
2.	L	S	Fwd
3.	R	q	Bwd
4.	L	q	Sd
5.	R	S	Dr

Teaching Hints

The man must adjust the length of his steps to lead the woman's turn. His steps should be slightly smaller, and he must continue traveling forward as he turns the woman under his left arm to maintain a feeling of oneness.

CROSSOVER

Position—Closed to Semi-Open to Closed

Man's Part

	Foot	Rhythm	Direction	Lead
1.	L	S	Fwd	Body
2.	R	S	FwdX	RH Heel
3.	L	q	Sd	
4.	R	q	Cl	RH Fingertips
5.	L	S	Tc	

Woman's Part

	Foot	Rhythm	Direction
1.	R	S	Bwd
2.	L	S	FwdX
3.	R	q	Sd
4.	L	q	Cl
5.	R	S	Tc

Teaching Hints

Partners are in a Semi-Open Position in step 2 and immediately return to a Closed Position in step 3 where they remain until the end of the figure. With a strong lead from the man, the forward cross may be executed in step 4 as well.

RIGHT TURN

Position—Closed

Man's Part

	Foot	Rhythm	Direction	Lead
1.	L	S	Bwd (RTn)	RH Heel
2.	R	S	Fwd	RH
3.	L	q	Bwd	RH Palm
4.	R	q	Sd	
5.	L	S	Tc	

Woman's Part

	Foot	Rhythm	Direction
1.	R	S	Fwd (RTn)
2.	L	S	Bwd
3.	R	q	Fwd
4.	L	q	Sd
5.	R	S	Tc

Teaching Hints

Step 1 is a 90° turn and dancers should remember that the feet lead the direction of the turn. Dancers should first practice this figure individually, using the four walls as focal points to aid with direction. A good practice pattern when working in partners is: Tango Basic, Right Turn, Tango Basic, Right Turn.

LEFT TURN

Position—Closed

Man's Part

	Foot	Rhythm	Direction	Lead
1.	L	S	Fwd (LTn)	Body
2.	R	S	Bwd	RH Fingertips
3.	L	q	Fwd	
4.	R	q	Sd	
5.	L	S	Tc	

Woman's Part

	Foot	Rhythm	Direction
1.	R	S	Bwd (LTn)
2.	L	S	Fwd
3.	R	q	Bwd
4.	L	q	Sd
5.	R	S	Tc

Teaching Hints

On step 1 the man's left foot should be pointing outward while the woman's right foot points inward. This is a 90° turn which is executed on step 1, and a good practice pattern is to alternate between the Tango Basic and Left Turns.

ARGENTINE WALK

Position—Closed

Man's Part

	Foot	Rhythm	Direction	Lead
1.	L	S	Fwd	Body
2.	R	S	Fwd	
3.	L	q	Fwd	
4.	R	q	Sd	RH Palm

Woman's Part

	Foot	Rhythm	Direction
1.	R	S	Bwd
2.	L	S	Bwd
3.	R	q	Bwd
4.	L	q	Sd

Teaching Hints

As the dancers step sideward on the last quick step, each should allow the free foot to brush by the supporting foot in order to follow through into the next step. This prepares the dancers to either repeat this step or to comfortably begin any other.

BEGINNING ROUTINES

ROUTINE ONE

1. Travel
2. Tango Basic
3. Left Turn
4. Tango Basic
5. Left Turn
6. Basic Corté
7. Repeat in reverse direction

ROUTINE TWO

1. Tango Basic
2. Right Turn
3. Tango Basic
4. Right Turn
5. Travel (Fwd)
6. Travel (Bwd)
7. Repeat in reverse direction

ROUTINE THREE

1. Travel
2. Arch Turn
3. Travel
4. Argentine Walk
5. Argentine Walk
6. Right Turn
7. Right Turn
8. Repeat in reverse direction

ROUTINE FOUR

1. Argentine Walk
2. Crossover
3. Crossover
4. Travel
5. Arch Turn
6. Basic Corté
7. Repeat in reverse direction

ADVANCED SECTION

ADVANCED TRAVEL

Position—Closed to Semi-Open to Closed

Man's Part

	Foot	Rhythm	Direction	Lead
1.	L	S	Sd	RH Palm
2.	R	S	FwdX	RH Heel
3.	L	q	Fwd	Body
4.	R	q	Sd	RH Palm
5.	L	S	Dr	

Woman's Part

	Foot	Rhythm	Direction
1.	R	S	Sd
2.	L	S	FwdX
3.	R	q	Bwd
4.	L	q	Sd
5.	R	S	Dr

Teaching Hints

Dancers move into a Semi-Open Position on step 2 (FwdX) but immediately return to a Closed Position for the "Tango Close" (Fwd-Sd-Draw). A variation is to make a weight change on step 5 so that the entire figure can be repeated beginning with the opposite foot. This step may be verbally cued as shown above or by saying "Sd-Thru-Turn-Sd-Draw."

CORTÉ LEFT TURN

Position—Closed

Man's Part

	Foot	Rhythm	Direction	Lead
1.	L	S	Fwd	Body
2.	R	S	Bwd (LTn)	RH Fingertips
3.	L	q	Fwd	Body
4.	R	q	Sd	RH Palm
5.	L	S	Cl	

Woman's Part

	Foot	Rhythm	Direction
1.	R	S	Bwd
2.	L	S	IP (LTn)
3.	R	q	Bwd
4.	L	q	Sd
5.	R	S	Cl

Teaching Hints

The Corté is executed on step 1, recovering with a left turn of 90° on step 2. A variation is to use an Arch Turn on step 1, a Corté on step 2, and then to recover on the quick steps. If dancers make a weight change on step 5, the figure will repeat beginning with the opposite feet. If they only touch on step 5, it will simply repeat. This step becomes a right turning figure when the man leads his partner into a right turn on step 2. A 180° turn is possible on step 2 also. Leads must be strong to indicate direction.

THE FASCINATION

Position—Closed to Semi-Open to Closed

Man's Part

	Foot	Rhythm	Direction	Lead
1.	L	S	Sd	RH Palm
2.	R	S	FwdX	RH Heel
3.	L	q	Fwd (LTn)	RH Fingertips
4.	R	q	Fwd	Body
5.	L	S	Sd (RTn)	RH Palm
6.	R	-	Tc	

Woman's Part

	Foot	Rhythm	Direction
1.	R	S	Sd
2.	L	S	FwdX
3.	R	q	Fwd (RTn)
4.	L	q	Fwd
5.	R	S	Sd (LTn)
6.	L	-	Tc

Teaching Hints

Here again, the turns are 90°, and as this step repeats, it will move in the same direction since there is no weight change on step 6. Dancers may experiment with inserting 180° turns on steps 3 and 5. Note that steps 2, 3, and 4 are done in semi-open position.

ADVANCED CORTE

Position—Closed to Right Side

Man's Part

	Foot	Rhythm	Direction	Lead
1.	L	q	Fwd	Body
2.	R	q	Sd	RH Palm
3.	L	S	Bwd	RH Palm
4.	R	S	Fwd	Body
5.	L	q	Fwd	Body
6.	R	q	Dr	

Woman's Part

	Foot	Rhythm	Direction
1.	R	q	Bwd
2.	L	q	Sd
3.	R	S	Fwd
4.	L	S	Bwd
5.	R	q	Bwd
6.	L	q	Dr

Teaching Hints

As the man steps forward on the first step, he must turn slightly to his left to lead the woman into the Right Side Position. On any Corté, the knees must be relaxed, and each dancer must support his or her own weight. The man must be careful not to lead his partner so strongly that she loses her balance.

FAN

Position—Right Side to Closed

Man's Part

	Foot	Rhythm	Direction	Lead
1.	L	q	Fwd (LTn)	Body, RH Fingertips
2.	R	q	Sd	RH Palm
3.	L	S	Bwd (RTn)	RH Palm
4.	R	S	Fwd	Body
5.	L	q	Fwd (LTn)	RH Fingertips
6.	R	q	Dr	

Woman's Part

	Foot	Rhythm	Direction
1.	R	q	Bwd (LTn)
2.	L	q	Sd
3.	R	S	Fwd (RTn)
4.	L	S	Fwd
5.	R	q	Bwd (LTn)
6.	L	q	Dr

Teaching Hints

Steps 1, 3, and 5 call for pivot turns of 90° and a strong, firm lead by the man. As the man steps backward, he leads his partner forward and turns her at the same time. During this turn the man pivots on his left foot while the woman pivots on her right foot. Both partners step forward on the second slow step, assuming a Closed Position for the quick rock on the next quick steps. When repeated twice, this step ends up in the opposite direction.

ADVANCED ROUTINES

ROUTINE ONE

1. Advanced Travel
2. Advanced Travel
3. Corté Left Turn
4. Corté Left Turn
5. Fan
6. Fan
7. Repeat in reverse
   direction

ROUTINE TWO

1. Tango Basic
2. Corté Left Turn
3. Travel
4. Corté Left Turn
5. Tango Basic
6. Fascination
7. Fascination
8. Repeat in reverse
   direction

ROUTINE THREE

1. Fascination
2. Fascination
3. Advanced Corté
4. Advanced Corté
5. Argentine Walk
6. Argentine Walk
7. Repeat in reverse
   direction

ROUTINE FOUR

1. Fan
2. Fan
3. Advanced Corté
4. Corté Left Turn
5. Fascination
6. Fascination
7. Advanced Travel
8. Repeat in reverse
   direction

11

the polka

The Polka originated in Bohemia during the early nineteenth century, and for most of that century it enjoyed the participation of all levels of society throughout several countries of Europe. An early commentary about the Polka in the *Times* of London during the 1840s described it as encompassing the "intimacy of the Waltz combined with the vivacity of the Irish jig."

In the latter half of the nineteenth century, European immigrants introduced the Polka in the United States where it met with considerable censure. The intimacy and unrestrained enthusiasm of the dancers were considered irreligious and scandalous to a nation whose moral conduct was controlled in part by watchful, conservative religious groups. Nevertheless, the Polka endured, and today its exciting rhythm reverberates throughout the country, particularly in communities with strong European ties.

Generally, the Polka is considered a folk dance, but because of its appeal to students, teachers frequently include it in their ballroom dance instruction. The authors have found that the enthusiasm engendered by the Polka spawns a willingness to accept the challenges of style and form of more formal ballroom dancing.

TEMPO

The Polka is primarily a fast dance although some music is written at slower tempos. Initial lessons should be taught to music played at 100 to 120 beats per minute.

135

Once the basic steps are learned, the dancers will enjoy the more popular tempo of 120 to 140 beats per minute.

RHYTHM

The Polka is danced primarily to music written in 2/4 time, with the first beat more heavily accented in each measure. Occasionally a Polka tune is written in 4/4 time. Although there are several foot patterns, the Polka is danced generally to a quick, quick, slow (qqS) rhythm. Some Polka folk dances include changes of dance rhythm to accommodate the foot patterns of specific ethnic dances.

The music notation of the Polka is written in this manner:

qqS Rhythm

2/4							
Count	1	&	2&	1	&	2	&
Rhythm	q	q	S	q	q	S	

qqS Rhythm

4/4							
Count	1	2	3	4	1	2	3-4
Rhythm	q	q	S		q	q	S

STEPS

The following steps are included in the Polka:

Beginner's Section: Polka Basic, Travel Step, Left Turn, Right Turn, Chassé, and Semi-Open Walk

Advanced Section: Wheel, Arch, Crossover, Scissors and Weave

STYLING

The mood created by the music of the Polka seems to unleash new energies that unfortunately cause a display of configurations heretofore unseen on the ballroom floor. Too frequently, teachers allow their students to dance wildly about the floor with limited concern for proper styling of the Polka.

The Basic Polka Step is a hop-step-close-step pattern. Many dancers eliminate the hop and simply dance the step-close-step pattern, commonly called the Two Step.

The Polka is usually danced in accepted ballroom dance positions, although some dancers enjoy using dance positions more commonly employed in folk dance. Two popular positions are the Promenade and Shoulder-Waist Positions. (See photographs.)

Promenade Position

Shoulder-Waist Position

136

The Polka, although danced with less attention to formal ballroom styling, does follow the suggested points of good body position. The dancers should stand erect but slightly apart to allow for the leg raising action caused by the hop. Throughout the Polka, dancers commonly turn in a clockwise direction characterized by a pronounced sway to the right and then to the left. The sway is exaggerated by looking and leaning in the direction of the sway.

In summary, the Polka is a lively dance that frequently invites disregard for style and pattern. Dancers should try to capture the excitement of the Polka in a somewhat carefree but correct interpretation of the music.

TEACHING THE POLKA

Students love the Polka, and as a result, teachers enjoy teaching it. Occasionally such positive response to a specific dance form brings about a de-emphasis of another dance form. Certainly student enjoyment and interest are primary considerations for determination of course content, however, the teacher does have the responsibility to provide adequate time for each dance form.

The Polka is, indeed, a traveling dance. During group instruction each couple requires a minimum of ten square feet, and the instructor should organize the class so that the couples can move back and forth across the ballroom using combinations of traveling and turning steps.

Many beginning dancers have difficulty including the "hop" in the Polka Step. The teacher, therefore, should begin instruction with the Two Step. Once the class masters the Two Step and begins to move freely with confidence and expression, the dancers will respond more exactly to the demanding rhythm of the Polka by naturally including a slight hop or kick. Too frequently, teachers belabor the hop and retard the students' natural response to the music.

Initial lessons should begin with the couples in the Shoulder-Waist Position. This position allows the dancers to move freely and to assist each other as they learn the basic rhythm. As soon as the students learn the basic rhythm, the teacher should begin teaching specific steps in suggested ballroom dance positions. Throughout all lessons the teacher must remind the students about dancing courtesy. As in other dance forms rudeness is inexcusable in the Polka. For this reason, the authors suggest that instruction in more formal ballroom dances precede the Polka, thereby making the students more conscious of proper style and manner.

Cuing the Polka is similar to cuing other dance forms. The rhythmic, foot, and directional cues provided for each step should enable the teacher to instruct the class while simultaneously attending to the learning difficulties of individuals. There is a uniqueness about each dance form that frequently necessitates additional descriptive cues. Helpful cues for turning steps in the Polka are Left-Two-Three-And, Right-Two-Three-And, and Two-Step-Left-And, Two-Step-Right-And. The alert, attentive teacher constantly searches for more descriptive verbal cues that prompt the dancers to move smoothly and accurately from one dance step to another.

BEGINNING SECTION

POLKA BASIC

Position—Closed

Man's Part

	Foot	Rhythm	Direction	Lead
1.	R	-	Hp	
2.	L	q	Fwd	Body
3.	R	q	Cl	
4.	L	S	Fwd	
5.	L	-	Hp	
6.	R	q	Bwd	RH Palm
7.	L	q	Cl	
8.	R	S	Bwd	

Woman's Part

	Foot	Rhythm	Direction
1.	L	-	Hp
2.	R	q	Bwd
3.	L	q	Cl
4.	R	S	Bwd
5.	R	-	Hp
6.	L	q	Fwd
7.	R	q	Cl
8.	L	S	Fwd

Teaching Hints

Dancers may wish to be slightly apart when dancing the Polka in Closed Position. Many dancers simply Two Step when dancing forward or backward; they then dance the Polka Step in the more open positions and during turning steps.

TRAVEL

Position—Closed

Man's Part

	Foot	Rhythm	Direction	Lead
1.	R	-	Hp	
2.	L	q	Fwd	Body
3.	R	q	Cl	
4.	L	S	Fwd	
5.	L	-	Hp	
6.	R	q	Fwd	Body
7.	L	q	Cl	
8.	R	S	Fwd	

Woman's Part

	Foot	Rhythm	Direction
1.	L	-	Hp
2.	R	q	Bwd
3.	L	q	Cl
4.	R	S	Bwd
5.	R	-	Hp
6.	L	q	Bwd
7.	R	q	Cl
8.	L	S	Bwd

Teaching Hints

Because of the knee-raising action caused by the hop of the Polka Step, it may be advisable to Two Step during this dance step. If the dancers choose to use the Polka Step, they should move apart slightly during this step.

LEFT TURN

Position—Closed

Man's Part

	Foot	Rhythm	Direction	Lead
1.	R	-	Hp	
2.	L	q	Fwd (LTn)	Body
3.	R	q	Cl	
4.	L	S	Fwd	
5.	L	-	Hp	
6.	R	q	Bwd (LTn)	RH Fingertips
7.	L	q	Cl	
8.	R	S	Bwd	

Woman's Part

	Foot	Rhythm	Direction
1.	L	-	Hp
2.	R	q	Bwd (LTn)
3.	L	q	Cl
4.	R	S	Fwd
5.	R	-	Hp
6.	L	q	Fwd (LTn)
7.	R	q	Cl
8.	L	S	Fwd

Teaching Hints

Beginning dancers should complete a 90° turn during this step. Advanced dancers should be able to turn 180°. Dancers should look in the direction of the turn. Dancers may wish to be slightly apart for this step if they do the Polka Step.

RIGHT TURN

Position—Closed

Man's Part

	Foot	Rhythm	Direction	Lead
1.	R	-	Hp	
2.	L	q	Sd (RTn)	RH Heel
3.	R	q	Cl	
4.	L	S	Sd	
5.	L	-	Hp	
6.	R	q	Sd (RTn)	RH Heel
7.	L	q	Cl	
8.	R	S	Sd	

Woman's Part

	Foot	Rhythm	Direction
1.	L	-	Hp
2.	R	q	Sd (RTn)
3.	L	q	Cl
4.	R	S	Sd
5.	R	-	Hp
6.	L	q	Sd (RTn)
7.	R	q	Cl
8.	L	S	Sd

Teaching Hints

This is a very popular step that is more attractive when performed with the Polka Step rather than the Two Step. The side steps (2 and 4) of the man are slightly forward, whereas the side steps (6 and 8) are slightly backward. The side steps of the woman are initially backward and then forward. There is a pronounced sway to the left on step 2, and to the right on step 6. Dancers should look in the direction of the sway. (See photographs.)

Right Turn

CHASSÉ

Position—Closed

Man's Part

	Foot	Rhythm	Direction	Lead
1.	R	-	Hp	
2.	L	q	Sd	RH Palm
3.	R	q	Cl	
4.	L	S	Sd	
5.	L	-	Hp	
6.	R	q	Sd	RH Palm
7.	L	q	Cl	
8.	R	S	Sd	

Woman's Part

	Foot	Rhythm	Direction
1.	L	-	Hp
2.	R	q	Sd
3.	L	q	Cl
4.	R	S	Sd
5.	R	-	Hp
6.	L	q	Sd
7.	R	q	Cl
8.	L	S	Sd

Right Turn

Teaching Hints

Dancers frequently use this step to recover from the exhaustive traveling and turning steps. The Chasse is more attractive if the dancers assume a more face-to-face (conversation) position rather than the Closed Position.

SEMI-OPEN WALK

Position—Semi-Open

Man's Part

	Foot	Rhythm	Direction	Lead
1.	R	-	Hp	
2.	L	q	Fwd	RH Palm
3.	R	q	Cl	
4.	L	S	Fwd	
5.	L	-	Hp	
6.	R	q	Fwd	RH Palm
7.	L	q	Cl	
8.	R	S	Fwd	

Woman's Part

	Foot	Rhythm	Direction
1.	L	-	Hp
2.	R	q	Fwd
3.	L	q	Cl
4.	R	S	Fwd
5.	R	-	Hp
6.	L	q	Fwd
7.	R	q	Cl
8.	L	S	Fwd

Teaching Hints

This step is usually the easiest one to perform simply because the man is unconcerned about stepping on his partner's toes. The man must give a strong heel (RH) lead when moving from Closed Position into the Semi-Open Walk, and a strong fingertip (RH) lead when moving from this step to a dance step in the Closed Position. This step flows beautifully into a Right Turn.

BEGINNING ROUTINES

The following routines are designed to move the dancers back and forth across the ballroom floor.

ROUTINE ONE

1. Polka Basic
2. Polka Basic
3. Travel
4. Travel
5. Chassé
6. Chassé
7. Left Turn (90°)
8. Left Turn (90°)
9. Repeat in reverse direction

ROUTINE TWO

1. Chassé
2. Chassé
3. Travel
4. Travel
5. Polka Basic
6. Polka Basic
7. Right Turn (90°)
8. Right Turn (90°)
9. Repeat in reverse direction

ROUTINE THREE

1. Travel
2. Travel
3. Right Turn (90°)
4. Right Turn (90°)
5. Semi-Open Walk
6. Semi-Open Walk (to Closed Position)
7. Travel
8. Travel
9. Left Turn (90°)
10. Left Turn (90°)
11. Repeat

ROUTINE FOUR

1. Travel
2. Travel
3. Right Turn (90°)
4. Right Turn (90°)
5. Semi-Open Walk
6. Semi-Open Walk (to Closed Position)
7. Right Turn (90°)
8. Right Turn (90°)
9. Repeat

ADVANCED SECTION

Advanced dancers should be able to perform the following steps in the Two Step and Polka pattern. With the addition of the steps in this section, dancers should be able to arrange their repertoire of steps into attractive combinations.

WHEEL

Position—Right Side

Man's Part

	Foot	Rhythm	Direction	Lead
1.	R	-	Hp	
2.	L	q	Fwd	Body
3.	R	q	Cl	
4.	L	S	Fwd	
5.	L	-	Hp	
6.	R	q	Fwd	Body
7.	L	q	Cl	
8.	R	S	Fwd	

Woman's Part

	Foot	Rhythm	Direction
1.	L	-	Hp
2.	R	q	Fwd
3.	L	q	Cl
4.	R	S	Fwd
5.	R	-	Hp
6.	L	q	Fwd
7.	R	q	Cl
8.	L	S	Fwd

Teaching Hints

Basically this is a turning traveling step. It does require a strong fingertip (RH) lead if preceded by a step in Closed Position, and a strong heel (RH) lead if followed by a step in Closed Position. The man must turn sharply toward his partner if he wishes to follow the Wheel with a step in the Closed Position.

ARCH

Position—Arch to Semi-Open

Man's Part

	Foot	Rhythm	Direction	Lead
1.	R	-	Hp	
2.	L	q	Fwd	LH High & RH Palm
3.	R	q	Cl	
4.	L	S	Fwd	
5.	L	-	Hp	
6.	R	q	Fwd	
7.	L	q	Cl	
8.	R	S	Fwd	

Woman's Part

	Foot	Rhythm	Direction
1.	L	-	Hp
2.	R	q	Fwd (RTn)
3.	L	q	Cl
4.	R	S	Fwd (RTn)
5.	R	-	Hp
6.	L	q	Bwd (RTn)
7.	R	q	Cl
8.	L	S	Bwd (RTn)

Teaching Hints

During the Arch the man simply performs a Travel Step while his partner dances under an arch formed by his left and her right hand. The woman should travel down the line of dance as she turns, rather than simply turning in place. This step combines well with the Semi-Open Walk.

CROSSOVER

Position—Closed to Semi-Open

Man's Part

	Foot	Rhythm	Direction	Lead
1.	R	-	Hp	
2.	L	q	Fwd	Body
3.	R	q	Cl	
4.	L	S	Fwd	
5.	L	-	Hp	
6.	R	q	Fwd X	RH Heel
7.	L	q	Cl	
8.	R	S	Fwd	

Woman's Part

	Foot	Rhythm	Direction
1.	L	-	Hp
2.	R	q	Bwd
3.	L	q	Cl
4.	R	S	Bwd
5.	R	-	Hp
6.	L	q	FwdX
7.	R	q	Cl
8.	L	S	Fwd

Teaching Hints

Because of the fast tempo of the Polka, this step must be done with small steps. The Crossover concludes normally in the Semi-Open Position. However, if the man gives a strong heel (RH) lead on step 8, the couple can return to the Closed Position. This step flows naturally into the Semi-Open Walk.

SCISSORS

Position—Closed to Left Side to Right Side

Man's Part

	Foot	Rhythm	Direction	Lead
1.	R	-	Hp	
2.	L	q	FwdX	Body and RH Heel
3.	R	q	Cl	
4.	L	S	Fwd	
5.	L	-	Hp	
6.	R	q	FwdX	Body & RH Fingertips
7.	L	q	Cl	
8.	R	S	Fwd	

Woman's Part

	Foot	Rhythm	Direction
1.	L	-	Hp
2.	R	q	BwdX
3.	L	q	Cl
4.	R	S	Bwd
5.	R	-	Hp
6.	L	q	BwdX
7.	R	q	Cl
8.	L	S	Bwd

Teaching Hints

Throughout this step the dancers travel diagonally down the line of dance, first to the man's right and then to his left. The man moves from the left side to the right side of his partner as she continues to travel backward. To perform this step smoothly, the dancers should be slightly farther apart than normal.

WEAVE

Position—Closed to Reverse to Semi-Open

Man's Part

	Foot	*Rhythm*	*Direction*	*Lead*
1.	R	-	Hp	
2.	L	q	Fwd X	RH Fingertips
3.	R	q	Cl	
4.	L	S	Fwd	
5.	L	-	Hp	
6.	R	q	Fwd X	RH Heel
7.	L	q	Cl	
8.	R	S	Fwd	

Woman's Part

	Foot	*Rhythm*	*Direction*
1.	L	-	Hp
2.	R	q	Fwd X
3.	L	q	Cl
4.	R	S	Fwd
5.	R	-	Hp
6.	L	q	Fwd X
7.	R	q	Cl
8.	L	S	Fwd

Teaching Hints

This step requires a strong, timely fingertip (RH) lead to move the dancers from Closed to Reverse Position and a strong heel (RH) lead to move them from the Reverse to Closed Position. Some men find it easier to enter the Weave by preceding it with one Polka step forward so that they can begin the Weave on step 5. As a change in style, the dancers may choose to use the Full-Open Position instead of the Semi-Open Position.

ADVANCED ROUTINES

These routines are designed to move the couples back and forth across the ballroom floor. They include combinations of beginning and advanced steps.

ROUTINE ONE

1. Travel
2. Travel
3. Wheel (180°)
4. Wheel (180°)
5. Polka Basic
6. Polka Basic
7. Right Turn (180°)
8. Repeat in reverse direction

ROUTINE TWO

1. Travel
2. Travel
3. Scissors
4. Scissors
5. Polka Basic
6. Polka Basic
7. Left Turn (90°)
8. Left Turn (90°)
9. Repeat in reverse direction

ROUTINE THREE

1. Polka Basic
2. Polka Basic
3. Scissors
4. Scissors
5. Travel
6. Travel
7. Semi-Open Walk
8. Arch
9. Semi-Open Walk (to Closed)
10. Right Turn (180°)
11. Repeat in reverse direction

ROUTINE FOUR

1. Travel
2. Travel
3. Weave
4. Weave
5. Travel
6. Travel
7. Crossover
8. Semi-Open Walk
9. Right Turn (180°)
10. Repeat in reverse direction

bibliography

Books

Astaire, Fred. *Steps in Time.* New York: Harper and Brothers, Publishers, 1959.

Bernstein, Martin, and Picker, Martin. *An Introduction to Music.* Englewood Cliffs: Prentice-Hall, Inc., 1972.

Borrows, Frank. *Theory and Techniques of Latin-American Dancing.* London: Frederick Muller Limited, 1964.

Chujoy, Anatole. *The Dance Encyclopedia.* New York: A. S. Barnes and Company, Inc., 1949.

Day, Mel, and Day, Helen. *Easy Cues for Ballroom Dances.* 1120 Longmont Street, Boise, Idaho.

Fletcher, Beale. *How to Improve Your Social Dancing.* New York: A. S. Barnes and Company, Inc., 1956.

Franks, A. H. *Social Dance—A Short History.* London: Routledge and Kegan Paul, 1963.

Hall, J. Tillman. *Dance!* Belmont, California: Wadsworth Publishing Company, Inc., 1959.

Harris, Jane; Pittman, Anne; and Waller, Marlys S. *Dance A While.* Minneapolis: Burgess Publishing Company, 1969.

Haskell, Arnold. *The Wonderful World of Dance.* London: L.T.A. Robinson Ltd., 1960.

Heaton, Alma. *Ballroom Dance Rhythms.* Dubuque, Iowa: William C. Brown Company, 1969.

————. *Techniques of Teaching Ballroom Dance.* Provo, Utah: Brigham Young University Press, 1965.

Howard, Bertrand. *Fundamentals of Music Theory: A Program.* Chicago: Harcourt, Brace and World, Inc., 1966.

Kraus, Richard G., and Sadlo, Lola. *Beginning Social Dance.* Belmont, California: Wadsworth Publishing Company, Inc., 1964.

Meerloo, Joost. A. M. *The Dance, from Ritual to Rock and Roll—Ballet to Ballroom.* Philadelphia and New York: Chilton Book Company—Book Division, 1960.

Moore, Alex. *Ballroom Dancing.* London: Pitman Publishing, 1974.

Morton, Virgil L. *The Teaching of Popular Dance.* New York: J. Lowell Pratt and Company, 1966.

Murray, Arthur. *How to Become a Good Dancer.* New York: Simon and Schuster, 1959.

Parson, Thomas E. *How to Dance.* New York: Barnes and Noble, Inc., 1960.

Pillich, William F. *Social Dance.* Dubuque, Iowa: William C. Brown Company, 1967.

Riel, Fran, and Davis, Beulah. *Happy Dancing: Handbook of Dance Mixers.* Minneapolis: Burgess Publishing Company, 1966.

Rosanova, Angela M. *Ballroom Dancing Made Easy.* New York: Vantage Press, Inc., 1954.

Sachs, Curt. *World History of the Dance.* New York: W. W. Norton and Company, Inc., 1937.

Shanet, Howard. *Learn to Read Music.* New York: Simon and Schuster, 1967.

Villacorta, Aurora. *Step by Step to Ballroom Dancing.* Danville: The Interstate Printers and Publishers, Inc., 1974.

White, Betty. *Ballroom Dancebook for Teachers.* New York: David McKay Company, Inc., 1962.

————. *Latin American Dance Book.* New York: David McKay Company, Inc., 1958.

Youmans, John G. *Social Dance.* Pacific Palisades, California: Goodyear Publishing Company, Inc., 1969.

Record Companies

Capitol Records, Hollywood, California.

Columbia Records, 1473 Barnum Avenue, Bridgeport, Connecticut.

Decca Records, A Division of MCA Inc., New York, New York.

Educational Activities, Inc., P.O. Box 392, Freeport, New York 11520.

Educational Dance Recordings, Inc., P.O. Box 6062, Bridgeport, Connecituct.

Grenn, Inc., P.O. Box 16, Bath, Ohio.

Herbert, 1657 Broadway, New York, New York 10019.

Hoctor Educational Records, Inc., Waldwick, New York 07463.

Kimbo Educational Records, P.O. Box 55, Deal, New
    Jersey 07723.
MacGregor Records, 729 South Western Avenue, Holly-
    wood, California.
Telemark Dance Records, Box 55, McLean, Virginia 22101.
Victor Records Radio Corporation of America, Camden,
    New Jersey.
Windsor Records, 5528 North Rosemead Blvd., Temple
    City, California.

Sources of Ballroom Dance Material

Dance Caravan Productions, 250 West 57th Street, Room
    929, New York, New York 10019.
Heaton, Alma, 273-H Richards Bldg., Brigham Young
    University, Provo, Utah 84601.
Imperial Society of Teachers of Dancing, United States
    Branch, George Elliot, General Secretary, 1319 20th
    Avenue, San Francisco, California.
United States Ballroom Council, 268 West 47th Street,
    New York, New York, 10036.
United States and World Dance News, 1336 New York
    Avenue N.W., Washington, D.C. 20005.